ABOUT THE AUTHOR

David J. Petry

Dave Petry is obsessed with making the most of his time here on Earth. He's written over a dozen books, written and recorded more than one hundred songs, plays over a dozen instruments, is a pilot, public speaker, teacher and entertainer! He has 3 children and has been married to his lovely wife Diane for more than twenty years.

Dave's writings are inspired by his experiences in life of traveling to all 50 states, more than 30 countries, and snorkeling at over 50 scenic sites throughout the world. He has a passion for eclectic taste in reading and conversation. After spending over thirty years as a research development mechanic, he changed careers and now spends his days helping at a retirement center working with the elderly. When asked how this is working out he replies, "I'm the happiest I've ever been in my life and having 'Rock Star Status' at a retirement home is better than no rock star status at all."

"Life is too short to sit around and be miserable."
David J. Petry

BOOKS BY THE AUTHOR

The Children of the Chiefs
A physics student goes back in time to warn the Native Americans.

Science Fiction, Murders, Mysteries, and Adventures
BOOK ONE
Thought provoking short stories.

Science Fiction, Murders, Mysteries, and Adventures
BOOK TWO
More thought provoking short stories.

SKY QUEEN: Becoming a private pilot
A Recipe to Relieve Stress
How to become a pilot, and some interesting flying stories.

PROZAC ATTACK
Laugh, Don't Cry
This is for people who dare to enjoy the humor of life. Laughter is "A Recipe to Relieve Stress!"

Get Serious
UFOs, alternative histories, theories of politics, religion, philosophies and more.

The Retirement Center
Fact is funnier than fiction, and more entertaining.

GULLIBLE'S TRAVELS
Around the World in Fifty Years
Travel is my hobby and it's always educational and hilarious.

The Chilling Adventures of Nick Sabo
What's it like for a young boy to encounter horrors at every turn?

Take What You Want and Leave the Rest Bible Study
Honest study of the scriptures.

124 SONGS YOU'VE NEVER HEARD
Guitar chords and lyrics to the songs of Dave and Bob.

Cheaper by the Dozen
This is what every family should do for future generations.

Custom Monster Models
How to build them and Dave's model building tips.

Bible of Model Rocketry
Draw from the wealth of over 800 launches and 100 rockets.

BIBLE OF MODEL ROCKETRY
By David J. Petry

TABLE OF CONTENTS

"You know...old folks can have dreams too, as well as young folks, and then work toward them. And to have a dream like this come true for me is just a terrific experience."
John Glenn

SPACE TAXI

INTRODUCTION

Many people look at the Bible as a guide for their spiritual journey on earth. It's a book of answers, filled with wisdom and knowledge for people of all ages to hopefully find their way through life.

This book is a guide of wisdom and knowledge for any man, or woman, or boy, or girl, or…that has an interest in the wonderful hobby of model rocketry. Life is full of trials and errors. Building rockets is no exception. Just as the book of Jasher and Enoch are missing from the scriptures, I'm sure there will be questions unanswered when you've turned the last page. The Bible says we shouldn't add or take away from the scriptures. This isn't a holy book. You can add your knowledge and leave behind whatever seems to be of no use. I've probably forgotten more than most people have learned about model rocketry…what were we talking about?

Hopefully, many of the tips I'd like to share will keep you from making the same mistakes I've made over the years and if you have as much fun as I've had over the years, you are a blessed individual.

This book is not a dictionary and its purpose is *not* to tell you what a launch lug is. After you build and launch a few rockets, most all of this book will make complete sense. The instructions that come with the kits are very good and they give one a basic education of the components needed to build them correctly. All one needs to do is go to the Internet and do a Google search of

"Estes model rocket catalogs." A number of websites will pop up and you can download old catalogs for free. They will show detailed diagrams and pictures describing the ins and outs of the hobby and you can see all of the wonderful kits from over the past years. The pictures in the catalogs are the property of Estes and cannot be displayed without permission.

Advanced Model Rocketry will not be covered in this edition. Using engines above an "E", or radio controlled gliders are a level above the *garden variety* of shooting off rockets.

There are a number of David J. Petry commandments. Just as one should take head when reading "Thou shalt not kill," or "Thou shalt not steal," so should the reader pay close attention to the rocket commandments.

Another noteworthy thing to pay close attention to is when meeting my friend Mr. Ever. His first name is Hal…Hal Ever. But he spells his name differently when trying to teach students words of wisdom. Mr. Ever shows up on a regular basis and when he does, his name is spelled, HOWEVER. Take heed when you see that word!

I've loved Star Trek from the time I saw the first episode as a young boy. In the original series, Captain Kirk would record important things in the CAPTAIN'S LOG, so we will too!"

There are references that say (See page …). If you're going to read the book cover to cover, feel free to ignore them; HOWEVER, if you're cross referencing a subject, it is very important to key off of the different pages that share things about a specific related subject.

One day when I was twelve years old, a friend of mine said, "Let's go shoot off my rocket."

"You mean to tell me that it really flies?" I asked.

"We'll find out!" he replied.

Grabbing some matches and a fuse, we headed for a clearing beside the road in front of his house. There wasn't much traffic back then. His launch system was extremely basic. He shoved a straightened out coat hanger in the ground, and then slid the rocket onto his homemade launch rod after jamming a fuse into the bottom of the engine. "Get ready to run!" he said while squatting down and lighting a match. When he jumped back and ran about fifteen feet from the rocket, I followed.

It shot up in the air a few hundred feet and then the parachute opened. The two of us kept an eye on it and as sure as the world turns, it landed in the street and broke a fin or two. I thought it was a great experience, but couldn't begin to entertain any ideas of getting into such a hobby, for the reason that I had no money.

That changed when I was all grown up and had two sons. This was my opportunity in life to get into some things I missed out on as a child, and I could use the excuse that those things were for my boys. We got a road race set and the US Trucker layout, however, buying and building model rockets was on the top of the list.

I didn't have a clue of how to do anything related to the hobby when buying the first kit. We started out with a few simple ones and then progressed up the most complicated kits and eventually I began building prototypes and doing experimentations of different kinds.

My occupation gave me an enormous advantage toward building and launching rockets. I was a research development mechanic making prototypes for a chemical valve company. This required using many types of machinery and test equipment and a little welding on the side, while working with exotic plastics and metals. I had also built more than a hundred plastic models over the years, so that experience helped immensely.

The kids eventually lost interest; nevertheless, the more I delved into things the greater my interest increased. It's actually not kid stuff! The rockets must be built and launched correctly to operate successfully and the fundamental building blocks are the same ones used by NASA. A rocket is a rocket!

It's time for me to come out of the closet and admit to the world, "I'm a big kid at heart and if building and shooting off rockets is kid stuff…then I'm never going to grow up!"

"Thou shalt buy a starter kit for thy first rocket so thou hast all the components needed to get started."
(E.g. launch pad, engines, rocket, and instructions)

CAPTAINS LOG: Star date 2114.1, "We are orbiting the planet Crouton. This should be interesting. I think we're about to have a wonderful adventure."

Chapter One
ROCKET HISTORY

Archytas, a Greek man from the city of Tarentum, all the way back in 400 BC, gets credit for the first rocket. He took a wooden pigeon, suspended it from a wire and with steam power, propelled it far enough to be given credit for discovering a new form of technology. It was similar to a balloon rocket where one builds a rocket out of a tube, suspended from a wire and then by putting a balloon inside of the tube, you blow it up and when you let go, the air power drives the rocket. If they had latex balloons back then he probably would have used one of them.

In the first century AD, the Chinese made a basic "chemistry set" gunpowder out of saltpeter, sulphur, and charcoal. (We did plenty of that as kids without our parents knowing about it.) They would put gunpowder into pieces of bamboo and throw them into the fire. It would explode and that got peoples attention, so it was a popular thing at religious festivals. (If you try that at church next Sunday, it may not go over very well.)

Next, someone got a great idea of tying those Chinese M80s to arrows, lighting them up and shooting them off. Eventually it evolved to launching the firecrackers like modern bottle rockets. In 1232 the Chinese fired a barrage of them at the Mongols during a war. They didn't do overwhelming damage physically, but the psychological effect was rather effective.

As with most wars, it's not long before the enemy duplicates *your* new technology. The

Mongols thought it was a great idea and improved upon it for decades and later from the 13th to the 15th century spread their rocket technology throughout Europe.

A monk from England by the name of Roger Bacon experimented with gunpowder and improved it greatly, giving the rockets a much longer range. Then a Frenchman named Jean Froissart figured that if the rockets were launched from a tube (like a modern fireworks rocket-launcher) they could more accurately hit a target. His device became the basis of the bazooka.

By the 16th century rocket warfare was listed as ineffective and its use reverted back to being used as fireworks for amusement. And then a German fellow named Johann Schmidlap (say that six times in a row very swiftly) invented a system of launching a two-staged rocket that became the basis of our modern rocket program.

There's a legend that a famous Chinese fellow rigged up a chair with two kites and 47 rockets tied to arrows. He was going to join Elijah in the sky with his fiery chariot. They ignited the rockets and it's said that the whole project blew up and they never saw Wan Hu again. He just went up in smoke with the rest of his rocket ship and never saw Elijah or any other saints in the Bible.

In 1792, and again in 1799, some people in India decided it was time for the British to go back and drink their tea in England, so they launched an enormous amount of rockets at the British, who were under the command of Colonel William Congreve. He liked the idea so much that he pushed for the British to start building rockets. They were used in the war of 1812. That's what inspired Francis Scott Key to write, "the rockets red glared" in his song "The Star Spangled Banner."

Along came a fellow by the name of William Hale. He'd never seen an Estes rocket kit because they weren't in business yet. He couldn't buy the Spin Fin rocket, so he made his own, and discovered that it worked like rifling in a cannon or modern pistol. It increased the accuracy of rockets. As things progressed, they lost their effectiveness when coming up against the Prussian Breech-loading cannons with rifled barrels and exploding warheads.

In 1898 a Russian schoolteacher, Konstantin Tsiolkovsky, must have been entertaining the thought of writing science fiction novels because he came up with the idea of using rockets to go into outer space. He also concluded that liquid fuel rockets would be more efficient.

Along came Robert H. Goddard. If you're going to be famous, always use a middle initial. It sounds much more impressive like...David J. Petry. He started experimenting with solid fuel rockets and published a pamphlet in 1919 entitled "A Method of Reaching Extreme Altitudes." Goddard achieved the first successful liquid fueled rocket launch on March 16, 1926. "One small step for man...and a whole lot of liquid-oxygen and gasoline for mankind." It earned him the distinguished title of "The Father of Modern Rocketry."

Germany based their V2 technology on Goddard's work and improved upon it; however, they had the same problem as most others in history. Accuracy was a nasty beast to be conquered. Fortunately, their best scientist, Wernher von Braun, became the leader of the American program after the war. Both the Soviet Union and the United States realized that long-range intercontinental ballistic missiles were the future of weapons needed for world power.

The missiles were used for the early space programs of both countries. Before the United States launched astronauts with the Atlas and Redstone missiles, The Soviet Union, on October 4, 1957 launched an artificial satellite called Sputnik 1, and then later on put the first dog into outer space. Laika barked the Russian National Anthem until he ran out of oxygen and died seven days later.

Call us a copycat! On January 31, 1958, the United States launched Explorer 1 and shortly thereafter created NASA (National Aeronautics and Space Administration), a civilian agency, whose mission would be the peaceful exploration of space for the benefit of all humankind.

And then model rocketry became popular and the rest is history!

**This chapter was my own edited paraphrase from the NASA website on rocket history. It's only plagiarism if you're caught; otherwise it's called research.*

BASIC COMPONENTS OF A LAUNCH

1- Liftoff: The rocket takes off from the launch pad.
2- Acceleration: The rocket gains speed and climbs for altitude
3- Coasting and Tracking Phase: The rocket has used all of its fuel and is still gaining altitude.
4- Peak Altitude: The rocket reaches its highest altitude and is on its way down. The engine has a delay and then trapped air blows the cap off and pops the nose cone out of the rocket with a burst of smoke for tracking the rocket.
5- Recovery System Deployment: The parachute, streamer, or other recovery equipment is deployed and slows down the descent of the rocket.
6- Touchdown: The rocket lands on the ground (hopefully in one piece and not in a tree).

Chapter Two
TERMINOLOGY

ALTITRAK: A device that looks like a gun and is used to calculate the altitude of a rocket. It's one of the few ways to find out how high the rocket has gone and it works very well. The Altitrak is based on simple trigonometry. One need simply get a specific distance from the launch and get comfortable using it. Estes has done an excellent job in the manufacture of the device. It takes two people, because one person must launch the rocket while the other is positioned one or two hundred feet away. It comes with detailed instructions.

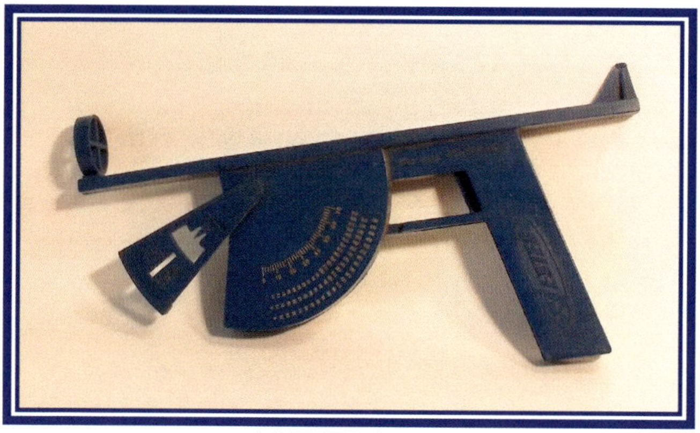

ALTITRAK

CAMERA ROCKETS: Years ago, Estes actually had a movie camera and they called it Cineroc. I'm sure it was interesting to use. They also had a nose cone that took one picture, called Camroc. They had their own rockets made specifically for the weight and design of the cameras. By the time I started building rockets they had the Astrocam. It used a 110 cartridge and would take as many pictures as was on the roll. It required 400-speed film, because of the motion involved, and did an outstanding job of taking pictures, but would only take one per launch. My first AstroCam was lost in a tree on a somewhat windy day.

That's the trouble with rockets. It's similar to being in high school and having the *hots* for someone. Part of you thinks, *I should wait to call, so it doesn't seem like I can't live without that man or woman;* nevertheless, the next thing you know, you're dialing the number.

I can't count how many times I should have stayed home because of the weather; HOWEVER, just like that phone call…the next thing I knew…there I was at the field shooting off—and losing another rocket!

A conservative spirit consumed me after I built my second AstroCam and I was much more careful when shooting it off. It worked great, but was an enormous challenge to build, because the two kits that I had required the rocketeer to build the camera. The B4-2 and C6-3 can leave you with pictures of the sky. The B4-4 and B8-5 engines are the best, because once the rocket is launched with a B6-6, the delay is long enough that the rocket picks up a considerable amount of speed and the camera can shred the parachute because of its weight. The C6-7 can shoot a good picture unless the wind claims it once the parachute opens, and the parachute can take a beating from the speed of the rocket.

Today there is the Estes Oracle Digital Video Rocket. It sells for close to $100.

ASTROCAM with LANTERN BATTERY LAUNCH PAD

ASTROCAM
Construction Area

ASTROCAM
Football Field

ASTROCAM
Neighborhood

CENTER OF GRAVITY
CENTER OF PRESSURE

CENTER OF GRAVITY: The balance point of the rocket. The easiest test for the stability of a rocket is to take a piece of twine or fishing line and make a lasso, so you can slide it over the rocket. Lift the rocket in the air and slide the lasso up or down until the rocket is balanced.

Take a piece of masking tape and use it to keep the rocket from slipping out of the lasso. Now go outside and swing the rocket around as if you're going to lasso a baby calf. If it flies in a stable fashion you're fine; HOWEVER, if it sways and shifts in an unstable manner you probably need more weight in the nose cone, or a different fin configuration, or both. The problem arises when building short, stubby rockets. They usually need extra weight in the nose cone. A basic, long rocket usually has good balance.

Lay a pencil on a table toward the edge, so that the fins of the rocket can hang over the edge of the table. Lay the rocket on the pencil and move it until it's balanced like a teeter-totter. That's the center of gravity.

Now make a flat, cardboard cutout of the profile-shape of the rocket and lay it across the pencil. When it is balanced, that is the center of pressure.

The center of pressure must be a considerable distance below the center of gravity or else the rocket will be unstable. If the nose cone is made of balsa wood you can use larger eye hooks and tighten washers onto the nose cone with the eyehook. Put a little Elmer's glue on the eyehook before screwing it into the nose cone for a more secure and durable fit. If the nose cone is plastic you need to take clay and jam it into the top of it. This can be tricky if the nose cone isn't made to do that. You may need to drill a hole in the under part of the nose cone, being careful not to mess up where the parachute and shock chord fasten to it. Squirt a small amount of airplane glue into the hole, wait until it runs to the tip of the nose cone and then roll some clay in your hands, forming a long skinny snake, slide it in, and then take a dowel and push it into the top of the nose cone. If too much airplane glue is used it may damage the plastic because airplane glue melts some plastics. Balsa is very light. Plastic nose cones automatically give the rocket more stability.

The SR-71 is a gorgeous kit. A friend of mine built his according to the directions and it flew great—but it was on a calm day. That kit should never be flown when it's windy, because the rocket is too flat. Another drawback with the SR-71 is that one needs to, very carefully squeeze the parachute into the body tube, because it's a tight fit and when the chute opens it tends to tear the top of the rocket; HOWEVER, it sure makes for a good flight. I wish they'd make a bigger SR-71.

These two teen-agers at the church asked me to launch their rockets. They'd built them but had no launch system. We went up to the school and prepared their SR-71 on the launch pad. 4,3,2,1, blastoff!

It went about sixty feet in the air, arched like a monument in Saint Louis and nose-dived into the ground of the parking lot while still accelerating.

I looked over at them and said in a monotone, "Did you leave the weight out of the nose cone?"

They gazed at me as if I had a direct channel to Almighty God. "How did you know?"

Like I said, "I've forgotten more than...what were we talking about."

That weight in the nose cone was needed for the rocket to have the correct center of gravity in relation to the center of pressure. If in doubt on the stability of a rocket, add weight to the nose cone; HOWEVER, the more weight in the nose, the more stress on the parachute. If it's an Estes kit, or probably any store bought kit, they've already tested the safety of this subject for their rockets. It's when building custom-made prototypes (scratch built kits) that one needs to be careful in regards to this subject.

There's a reason why they put those nose weights in the kits. A fellow said his wife had him repair the vacuum cleaner. He took it apart, found a loose wire and reconnected it. He noticed there was a chunk of metal mounted to the base and thought it was a cheap ploy to make the buyer think he or she was getting a heavy-duty product. The man said he removed the weight, put the sweeper back together, plugged it in, turned it on and watched it take off across the living room until it yanked the chord out of the receptacle. He now understood what the chunk of metal was for.

Who said this hobby is for kids? I'm not a rocket scientist but...or am I?

"Thou shalt not leave parts out of a kit!"

CENTER OF GRAVITY

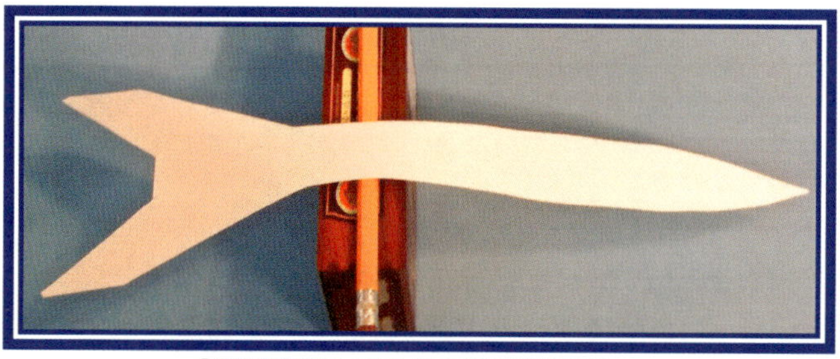

CENTER OF PRESSURE

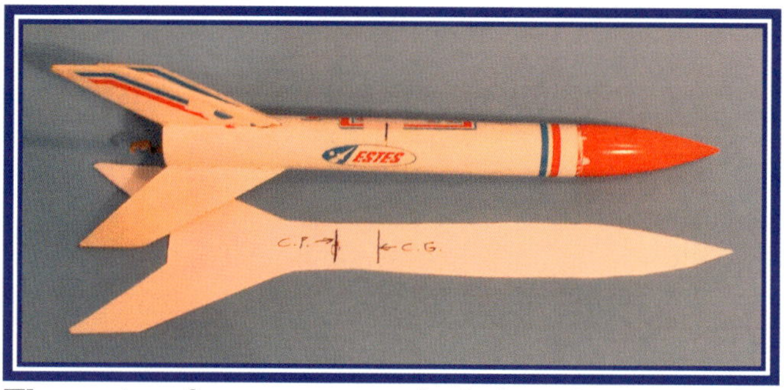

The center of pressure must be below the center of gravity for a stable flight.

DELAY times are extremely important and can be very attention grabbing. As was stated before, Estes does a good job on the recommendations for the first flight. Eventually I would shoot off rockets with engines that had delays long enough that the chute would open shortly before it hit the ground, so I could get the rockets back.

YES…there were times they nose-dived into the ground and it resulted in a damaged rocket. Don't take a chance of loosing the rocket too soon. Be conservative and get off a few launches that result in a successful recovery. After that, only if you can live with the fact that you may never see your hard work sitting on the shelf again, get risky and try engines that go high. Finding a wide-open field in Cincinnati is almost nonexistent.

The problem with long delays is that if the rocket is a heavy one, it will shred the parachute when it opens because of the velocity of the descending rocket. I had a D12-11 engine in one of the smaller "D" engine rockets. The nose cone never opened because it was going so fast that there wasn't enough power from the engine burst to blow the nosecone off.

A number of times I've had engines that malfunctioned and the nose cone didn't pop open. My first Mean Machine went from six feet in length—to three feet—in two seconds when it hit the ground. There was a group of kids watching and they couldn't stop laughing.

Things like that are funny when it's not your rocket. For years there was a R.C. air show in our area. They had all types of planes, jets, helicopters and the highlight of the show was a six-foot long space shuttle that was piggybacked on top of an enormous radio controlled aircraft. How the plane got off the ground is a question to be answered by its builder.

Once reaching the designated altitude, the plane would nose dive with a jerk and that would release the shuttle. The shuttle was a glider with a bunch of high-powered rocket engines that, when fired, shot it laterally across the sky and then when the rocket engines ran out of thrust, the pilot would glide it down and onto the runway. I saw it on Saturday and it was unforgettable.

The next day, on Sunday, they did a repeat performance. A fellow I worked with went to the show and when I saw him on Monday, he couldn't wait to tell me what had happened. He was laughing so hard that it took him ten minutes to get the entire story out and tears of laughter were in his eyes while he said, They were playing the "Star Spangled Banner" as the shuttle was ready to detach. It detached successfully and when the engines fired…it blew up into pieces. The only thing left was the nose of the shuttle floating to the ground.

Did I mention that rocket crashes are funny when it's not your rocket?

DESIGNER KITS: They are a must for the individual with a sense of adventure. Estes has had a number of them over the years and they are great fun for making your own ideas come to fruition. They have all of the components to build a variety of rockets and the builder can choose what to do with all of the parts.

Don't be bashful! You can buy regular kits and make changes as you see fit; HOWEVER, build a number of standard rockets before making your own. It's like all things in life; experience is the best teacher.

Back when I was building my new ideas, they had the "Designer's Special" and the "Futuristic Parts Assortment." They are a must for the serious, new-design rocket builder.

ENGINE ADAPTER: A device to interchange A, B, or C engines in a D engine casing. The V-2 goes very high with a "D" engine. If the field is small, it's better to use a C6-3 engine and this can be accomplished by using an adapter. The engine slides into the adapter and then the adapter is slid into the rocket.

A, B, C to D ADAPTER

The engine slides into the casing and the casing slides into the "D" sized engine casing of the rocket.

"Thou shalt not try to hold a rocket engine in thy hand when it has been ignited!"

CAPTAINS LOG: star date 2114.2, "Who's the idiot down in the engine room that tried to hold an engine in his hand?"

ENGINES: There must have been too much chlorine in the gene pool when God made the boy that lived up the street. He wanted to show how tough he was and to prove it, the kid held a rocket engine in his bare hand and had somebody ignite it. He lasted for a few seconds before dropping it, burning his hand badly and then crying like a baby from the pain.

Overall, the engines are very reliable. I've had some bad ones and have noticed that it's usually the entire package. While shooting off the Alpha 3 with an A8-3, the engine blew up and burnt a hole in the side of the rocket. It never left the launch pad.

Generally speaking, Estes has good recommendations on what engines to use. The first flight being the least powerful is excellent advice in regards to the prevention of losing one's rockets. I would be conservative with rockets and then when I felt I'd had my fun, it was time to "hang my hide out over the edge" and go for the gusto. I've lost many a rocket with that *cowboy* attitude, but it sure is exciting to fire a rocket off with a big engine.

The coding system is very simple. An "A" engine has a specific amount of dry fuel to lift the rocket. The "B" engine has twice as much fuel and power as the "A". The "C" engine has twice as much power as a "B" and the "D" engine has twice as much power as a "C". The "D" engine has a larger diameter and eight-times as much power as an "A" engine.

The "E" engine is twice as powerful as a "D", the same diameter—except it is longer, so the rocket must be built for the extra length. There is a spacer one can use if he or she chooses to launch the rocket with a "D" engine. The few rockets I've had that can use either engine, I built by gluing the spacer permanently into the rocket, since I don't buy or use "E" engines.

The next code is a number and it refers to the size of the nozzle. The larger the nozzle, the faster the dry fuel is released from the engine, so a large number wants to dump the fuel faster than a smaller number.

The third digit is also a number and it is the time of delay before the burst of air pops the nose cone off. An engine with the designation B6-4 has twice as much power as an "A" engine, with a size 6 nozzle and a 4 second delay.

An engine that is twice as powerful will not always make a rocket go twice as high. It will usually make it go much higher because it is accelerating at a faster speed for a longer duration of time. The Maxi-Alpha 3 is a big rocket and takes a recommended "D" engine. I didn't want to loose it on the first flight, so I used my "D" to "C" adapter and launched it straight in the air with a C6-3. It barely lifted off the ground, reached an altitude of about 80 feet and the parachute had only partially slowed down the rocket before it hit the ground. A fin broke and the body tube crimped slightly. On the next launch I put a D12-3 engine in it. The rocket went very high; probably 400 feet…and almost landed in a tree.

MINI ENGINES are fine and you get an extra engine for the money. A number of the kits are wonderful that take the mini engines; however, many of them have small body tubes and that means either a streamer or a small parachute must be jammed down inside the body tube. That can be a challenge at times.

The mini engines seem to have a few bad ones more often than the regular sized ones. While shooting off a three-stage rocket, with two A-0 booster engines, and then a final A8-3 engine, the engines didn't ignite the next stages properly. The rocket launched perfectly and went up about 100 feet, started falling out of the sky and turned 90 degrees. The second engine fired and it soared across the field like a fighter jet. When it ran out of fuel, the rocket was pointed at the ground and as it started to descend, the main engine fired. The rocket powered six inches into the soft, mushy ground. Wow...it was exciting!

I had a couple of packs of rocket engines that were all bad. It was the maiden launch of a freshly built rocket and it exploded on the launch pad and destroyed the rocket. I tried another engine on an expendable rocket and it also blew up. Next I took the last rocket engine, held in the vice on my workbench, stood back and ignited it. It also blew up.

I wrote to Estes and told them about it but they said I needed to send the rockets and engines to be reimbursed. I figured it wasn't worth spending money for the shipping cost and counted my losses.

The mini engines are a smaller diameter and the most powerful is an "A". They have a 1/2A, with half as much power and also a 1/4 A with one-fourth the power of an "A" engine.

CLUSTERS are about as tricky as it gets. I built an eight-foot rocket out of mailing tubes. Not to exaggerate, but it weighed at least a ton, (actually it weighed one pound). I clustered three

D12-3s in the bottom and used the battery on my car for the electrical supply. The igniters must be placed just so-so for it to work and then there are the six alligator clips. It is a real challenge to pull off—and expensive. The launch was spectacular, with three D engines straining to leave the bounds of earth behind. It reached an altitude of about 150 feet. (See U.S.S. Petry page 120).

The Saturn Five gave a choice of one D-12 engine, or a cluster of three C6-3s. The first time I shot it off with the cluster and everything went perfect. After that I decided to leave clustering behind. Too much can go wrong and it's a very time consuming ordeal.

MULTI-STAGING is exciting. I built a number of the multi-stage rockets. Some worked better than others. If the rocket engines touch each other they usually light the next stage without problem; however, some of the kits have a little too much distance between the rocket engines and I've had them fail to ignite the next stage.

With experimentation I found that one can simply tape the engines together with scotch tape and if the rocket is long enough, there is no need for extra fin units on the booster engines.
(See MULTI-STAGING page 110)

I personally prefer to, two stage rockets rather than cluster. Multi-stage launches are wonderful!

"Thou shalt take pictures and movies of thy launches whenever thou canst, or thou will wish thou did. Thy cell phone worketh greatly."

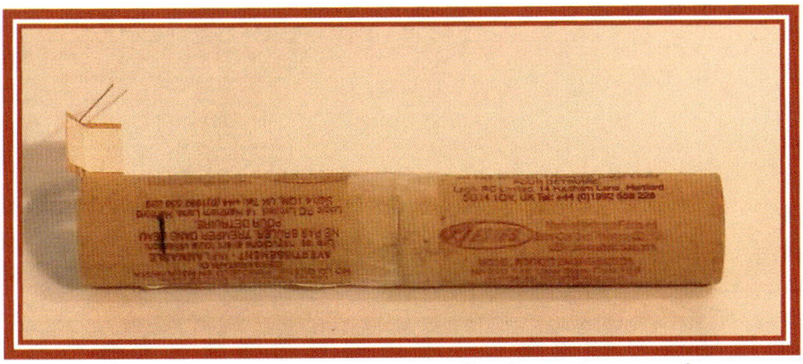

Use Scotch tape to connect the booster engine to the main engine.

IGNITERS: When we were kids, my friend would go to the hobby shop and buy a long strand of fuse. He'd cut off a piece a few inches long, shove it up the nozzle of the rocket engine, making sure it stayed in place, then he'd light it with a match and we would run. At that time the launch systems amounted to the electrical type sold today; however, the igniter was simply a piece of nichrome wire. The combination of not enough battery power, or the wire not being jammed up inside of the nozzle made it hard to accomplish a reliable lift off.

The fuse was a guaranteed ignition most every time…but not approved by NASA…or Estes.

When I began the hobby around 1980, Estes had developed the igniters with the gun power on the tip. They are very reliable unless the gunpowder has been damaged. They're very delicate and must be handled like a newborn baby. The more battery power you have, the better the launching results.

(See LAUNCH SYSTEMS page 42)

Do yourself a favor and buy extra igniters. There are usually six in a pack. Every now and then you'll have a bad one. Place the igniter into the nozzle, bend it at a ninety-degree angle and either place a small piece of masking tape over the bottom of the engine to hold it in, or use the little plastic plugs. They both work fine.

Observe the pictures and notice how I bend the wires into the air with a little separation, so they don't touch. Make sure you have a strong battery and clean alligator clips. Keep sandpaper on hand to clean the clips if necessary. Clip the piece of sandpaper into the alligator clip and pull it out. Do this repeatedly and your clips will be shiny and ready to go.

Estes plastic engine plugs hold the igniter in place. Notice the wires, up in the air and separated.

If you don't have the plastic plugs, or if they don't fit properly, use masking tape. Notice the wires turned up and separated.

FINISHES are very important if one wants to have top performance and a nice looking rocket sitting on the shelf. I did testing that proved, in some instances, that a rocket with balsa fins and a balsa nosecone, not painted or sanded, went more than twice as high after sanding, priming, and painting it with high gloss paint. In spite of the added weight of the paint, the elimination of an enormous amount of drag greatly increased the performance of the rocket.

(See DRAG pages 101, 103)

Kilz 2, a water-based primer found in most stores, works great on balsa wood. Sanding and painting multiple coats will ensure a nice surface to get a high gloss finish. Three or four coats, sanded lightly with fine sandpaper in between, brings forth an acceptable, finished product.

Rubbing alcohol, poured lightly on a wadded-up paper towel, and wiped on the entire surface of the rocket before painting should insure a good finish in regards to the paint. It removes oils and residues. Be very careful not to have the paper towel saturated because that can damage the cardboard tube.

The cheap brand of Wal-Mart spray paint usually works fine, except there are many colors they don't carry. Regardless of what brand you use, always use high gloss. The decals stick better to it and the finished product will be much better. If you want a flat finish, spray dull coat on the rocket as the final step.

Nothing on the market leaves a finished product equivalent to Testors gloss coat and dull coat. One thing to be careful of is decals. Make sure that the surface is shiny and smooth; HOWEVER, the gloss coat must be sprayed over the decals ever so lightly, with many coats, or they will bubble up. I've had excellent success with spraying Wal-Mart's cheap, clear spray paint on the rocket before and after the decals and then topping it off with a few coats of gloss coat. The decals don't seem to wrinkle as drastically with the Wal-Mart clear coat and once they have a few coats of it over top of them a person can spray a more liberal coat of Testors gloss coat for the finished product. Or dull coat if you want a flat finish, but dull coat will reduce the altitude of the rocket's performance.

Use some form of clear coat on all rockets. It protects the paint and if you use masking tape or anything that may damage the paint, the clear coat works as a first-line of resistance.

FINS can be a pain to glue to rockets. Estes makes a FIN ALIGNMENT GUIDE that works well; HOWEVER, I discovered that using a hot glue gun works great.

Make sure the grain of the wood is positioned correctly for maximum strength. It's amazing how a piece of balsa wood has almost no strength whatsoever, and will break by almost sneezing on it if the grain of the wood isn't glued correctly; HOWEVER, when the fin is positioned the correct way, there is plenty of strength. The rocket companies have already die-cut the balsa fins in the correct manner for this; HOWEVER, when making a scratch built model, make sure to get that grain in the right direction.

Using the hot glue gun is one of the biggest secrets of model building. The hot glue has no strength for long-term use when building rockets; HOWEVER, it works great as a tack welder to speed up the construction of gluing fins and launch lugs onto the body of a rocket.

The secret is to shoot a small amount at the top and bottom of a fin to be set in place and then quickly put pressure on the fin and hold it tightly in place for about a minute and then continue with all of the fins and launch lugs.

Now take the bottle of Elmer's glue and squirt a bead on all of the seam areas of the contact points of the fins and launch lugs where they touch the body. Once the glue dries the next day, repeat the Elmer's glue procedure. Let it dry another day. The finished result will have all the strength needed, the pieces will be in place and the builder will not be frustrated trying to hold the fins in place with the white glue alone.

The only drawback is that you'll see the spots where the hot glue was used, but with a little finesse it's barely noticeable.

Notice the beads of hot glue on the top and bottom of the fins and launch lug.

LAUNCH RODS AND LAUNCHPADS come in an assortment of arrangements. The tripod type (Porta Pad) that comes with many beginner kits is okay to start with; HOWEVER, they are much too light-duty for the bigger rockets.

My favorite was the type that bolted to a rectangular lantern battery. I now have a state-of-the-art, homemade launch pad that's easier on my back and safer, since a person can't bend over and poke their eye out if they forget to put the safety cap on the launch rod.

It's made from a cheap WORKMATE and a few pieces of scrap wood. The finished result is that it sits off of the ground, is very sturdy, and the rocket can easily be angled into the wind for a more dependable recovery.

"Thou shalt tape the launch rod to the launch pad with duct tape or masking tape."

The kit was a futuristic space station made by Centuri. It looked great except they have stick on decals that have a tendency to peel off. It was a heavy rocket and the weight of it cocked on the launch rod unawares to me. The rocket lifted off and took the launch rod with it. It did one of those Saint Louis Arch launches and slammed into the ground, with the launch rod still attached to the rocket. Had it hit someone, the emergency room would have been the next stop on the itinerary.

(See SATELLITE KILLER pages 68, 135)

I made my own launch pad, and again, being a research development mechanic for thirty-two years helped immensely. I took a piece of aluminum and drilled a hole that was a tiny bit bigger than the 3/16th rod. I then drilled and tapped a 10/24 thread for a set-screw to tighten from the side and put pressure on the launch rod.

Now I can use either sized launch rod. I store them in a piece of copper tubing with a cap on each end to keep them from getting bent.

Another advantage is that I have an automatic shoulder to keep the rocket off of the launch pad. When rockets sit on the launch pad, they can cock easier.

The uninformed rocketeer may not realize that the rocket does not push off of the pad. It will go at least the same altitude if it takes off at a higher spot on the launch rod.

A length of copper plumbing pipe, with a cap on each end, works excellent as a storage container for the 1/8th and 3/16th inch launch rods. They're worthless if bent. Bring along a can of 3 in 1 oil, light sandpaper, or steel wool to clean and lubricate the launch rod, and if you want to save your back and have more fun, purchase a cheap, lightweight workmate and make your own launch pad that can be gripped in the jaws.

CUSTOM LAUNCH PAD
With
MLAS Quest Mars Lander
Notice how it sits up, off of the launchpad.

One can adjust the angle very easily. It eliminates bending over and there is less chance of one poking their eye out on the launch rod. I prefer my paint-decal scheme over the original Maxi-Alpha 3

Notice the set screw that tightens down the launch rod. The blast shield is from the Dude and works nicely for all launches.

A 2x2 board is screwed to the plywood and the aluminum launch rod holder, with the set screw is bolted to the plywood.

LAUNCH SYSTEMS come in a number of variations. One of the popular ones is the small, hand held type that is powered by four AA batteries. The batteries don't last very long and the system isn't completely reliable.

One of the best ones over the years made use of a rectangular, six-volt lantern battery that became the launch pad. It gave weight to the launch pad and plenty of power.

The limitation of it is that the $3/16^{th}$ rod for the larger rockets won't slide into it; HOWEVER, I used my belt sander on the $3/16^{th}$ launch rod and VERY CAREFULLY ground it to an 1/8 of an inch, so it would fit into all 1/8 inch launch pads.

"If I were king…." all of the rockets would be built with $3/16^{th}$ launch lugs and there'd only be the $3/16^{th}$ rod."

Eventually I made my own launch system with a few parts from radio shack. Using the power source of a lantern battery will greatly increase many successful launches. I used the battery of my car at one time. "Talk about having all the power you need!"

Lately I have a "home made" launch system that is very reliable and perfectly safe if a person follows protocol.

I used a lantern battery and the alligator clips and wire that came with a starter kit. I then soldered alligator clips to the opposite ends, with a switch bridged on one of the wires. The switch is only "hot" when pushing it in. In between each launch I disconnect the alligator clips, so I have a *triple-safety* ignition system.

One needs to 1- connect the first alligator clip to the battery, 2- connect the second alligator clip to the switch, and 3- push the button in to launch the rocket.

I always do at least a five, four, three, two, one countdown when launching. If little kids are around, I always do a ten count. It can be interesting. "Ten, nine, eight, six, four, two, seven, two…"

At one time I rigged up an elaborate launch control with three lights that used an independent battery source for the LEDs. It was fancy and looked nice, but every extra link in the chain is another opportunity for failure.

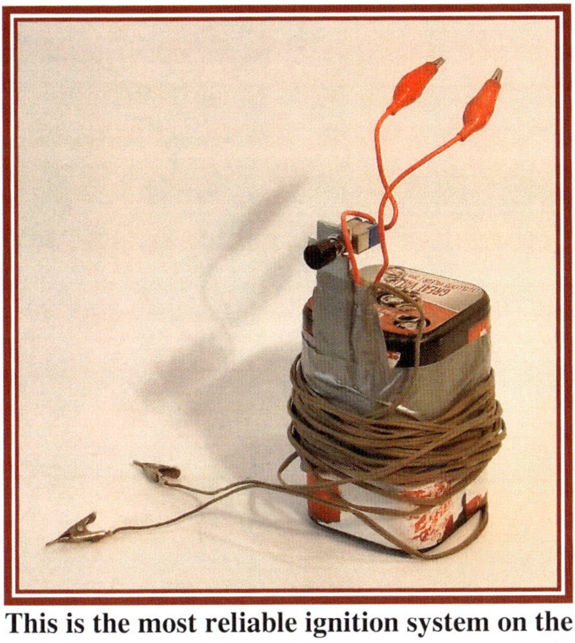

This is the most reliable ignition system on the market. It has a three-way safety sequence, so it's perfectly safe and has plenty of power.

PAYLOAD SECTIONS can be a lot of fun. My boys thought it was neat when we'd put Fisher Price plug people, or an action figure in the clear plastic payload section and shoot them off. Another neat thing about payloads is when you use a rocket that goes a few hundred feet on an "A" engine and 800 feet with a "C" engine. With the extra weight of a large payload, a "C" engine only lifts the rocket a few hundred feet. Everyone loves to see and hear a heavy liftoff.

The Bandit kit was extraordinary. It had a muffler system so it didn't need wadding.

Don't be bashful. If the payload section seems as if it wants to fall apart, before the launch, wrap a piece of masking tape around it to insure getting all of the pieces back. Before putting the masking tape on, use the *body shop* trick of touching the surface of the sticky part with your fingers. The oil from you skin will keep the tape from being overly sticky and it won't have as much of a tendency to peal off the shine—or worse yet, the paint.

The Scrambler works great and it had that heavy sound when it would lift off.

We haven't broken an egg yet!

Notice the masking tape that is holding the payload section together. This eliminates the probability of the pieces coming apart.

PURCHASING rockets can get expensive in a hurry. Fortunately, as far as hobbies go, rocketry is not ridiculous. Model railroaders can spend hundreds of dollars on a single locamotive engine. An R.C. aircraft pilot can drop hundreds of dollars buying an airplane in the blink of an eye. Going to the next level gets into thousands of dollars for many radio controlled kits.

How much does a man or woman shell out if they play on two golf leagues a week?

From experience, I've discovered that if you see a kit you like—buy it. Many rockets are discontinued if they don't sell well, or they may quit selling because they've been available for so long that everyone interested has already bought one.

I'm at a huge disadvantage. I love the space program. They no longer make the big Atlas rocket and a number of other's from over the years, so I can't purchase one. My only hope is eBay and when I find one, sometimes the seller is asking far more than I'm willing to pay.

If you see a kit you can't live without, buy it!

I've had much success buying models and rockets from online stores like Hobbylinc.com and Megahobbies.com; HOWEVER, you will need to pay for the shipping cost. Always check Amazon.com, because you can usually get free shipping on orders over twenty-five dollars. You'd be surprised at all of the products Amazon carries. Don't leave out eBay. I think that "The Dude" (Este's, over-seven foot rocket made from a Mylar tube) is one of the neatest rockets ever made. I picked one up on eBay for around twenty bucks and it was worth every *on-line* penny; HOWEVER, the shipping cost was high.

"Thou shalt use talcum powder on all parachutes and streamers."

RECOVERY SYSTEMS

STREAMERS: Talcum powder keeps the plastic from sticking to itself. If that happens, the streamer or parachute won't open and the rocket will come down much faster than designed, resulting in broken fins and other damaged components.

"Thou shalt check the ground and rocket to see if there are broken pieces lying around after recovery."

The most common mistake made with streamers is for them to fit so tightly into the body tube that they don't deploy and open up. If the streamer seems too tight, cut some of it off with a pair of scissors. It's better to have the rocket come down a little faster than expected rather than it fall from the sky with the streamer still stuck inside of the body tube.

I've had rockets rip apart because the parachute or streamer didn't deploy, so the rocket accepted the full impact of the discharge, resulting in the engine casing blowing out of the rocket, or the body tube ripping apart.

Make sure the nose cone doesn't fit too tight!

PARACHUTES: Most of the same applies to parachutes. Don't be bashful with the talcum powder. On extremely hot days, cold days, and especially humid days, plenty of talcum powder is required.

We had one humid day where, no matter what we did, it seemed as if the chutes did not want to open properly. The bigger rockets usually have parachutes and when they hit the ground hard they can end up with severe damage.

To increase the chances of recovering the rocket, a person can cut a hole in the top of the parachute. It will come down much faster; HOWEVER, it increases the chance of damage to the rocket. I had a three-stage rocket with a very basic design. It wasn't very heavy and I wanted it back. Recovering it with a broken fin was a more desired alternative than watching it drift into a neighborhood a mile away, never to be recovered. It had a 12-inch parachute. I cut a hole removing half of the parachute. The three-stage launch was spectacular and the rocket landed in the field and was easily recovered. Had I not tampered with the chute, it would have drift away to that resting place where rockets go when they die. There was no damage and we all lived happily ever after.

Ohio is heavily wooded. It's nearly impossible to find a place to launch rockets that can be safely retrieved without trees and power lines over a large area, unlike a desert in Arizona, so one must be selective of where and how the rockets are launched.

MULTIPLE PARACHUTES are a pain in the backside. It's hard enough to get a 24 inch parachute rolled up and stuffed into the body tube of some rockets; HOWEVER, getting two or three of them into the end of the rocket greatly increases the chance of them becoming tangled and not opening properly.

Use plenty of talcum powder and experiment with wrapping a sheet or two of toilet paper around each rolled up chute if there is enough room for both of them to slide comfortably into the body tube.

One of the greatest rockets ever designed is the Estes Saturn Five. Not only is it fantastic to view during a launch, if built and painted correctly, it looks impressive displayed in a room; HOWEVER, there are a number of engineering challenges related to it. The 24 inch parachutes are nearly impossible to get loaded when it comes time to squeeze them, and the nose cone, with its 10-inch parachute, into the body tube. (see SATURN FIVE page 118)

"Thou shalt paint featherweight rockets bright colors to aid in their recovery!"

FEATHERWIEGHT recovery is the most basic of all. Kits such and the Mosquito and the Streak are so small and light that after the engine pops out, they simply fall back to earth. The drawback with those rockets is that they shoot off so quickly one only sees a blur, and finding them at times can be nearly impossible, since there is no streamer or parachute to spot in the sky.

TUMBLE RECOVERY is a science all of its own. The Estes Scout was designed to do just such a thing. The rocket takes off very quickly, because it's very light, and then when the engine tries to eject, it slides part way out of the engine casing-body tube area, and is caught by an extended engine clip, causing it to tumble end over end and safely land in the field. The engine casing has enough weight to break a fin or two if it hits the blacktop, but if it lands in the grass that rascal can be shot off again and again.

After a number of victorious launches, it was time to load it with a C6-3 and kiss it goodbye. The Scout went so high that I lost sight of it and never did see that rocket again. Hopefully some kid found it before the rain rolled in.

"Your *attitude* limits your *altitude* in life." When losing a rocket, rather than fall into a depression, feel uplifted in the hopes that someone will find it before it's ruined by the weather. Look at it as if you're putting a donation in the offering plate and sharing your wealth with others for a good cause. (Have you read my book *Psychology 101 with David J. Petry*? You'll find it on the same shelf as my other book, *Humility, How I Got It*.) With rockets, "Your ALTITUDE can ruin your ATTITUDE if you lose the rocket."

"Thou shalt not launch any glider on a windy day!"

GLIDER recoveries are worthy of note. They must be built correctly. Their engineering is not what one would refer to as "garden variety." Before launching them up into the wild blue yonder, it's good to find soft-snow, or a field with high grass and throw it like a paper airplane to make sure the elevator and other control surfaces fly correctly.

It's better to have a mild nosedive, four feet off of the ground as opposed to 200 feet!

Most of them go up like a rocket and then a fin unit pops out and comes down with a parachute, while the wings snap open, making it a glider, and then it glides down successfully. One of the first such rockets was the Scissor Wing Transport.

The Crusader was stupendous. It was the next generation "Scissor Wing Transport" with much increased performance. Charity overcame me one day and I gave my Crusader to a friend. And I still wish I had kept it. "Give until it hurts!"

The Space Shuttle is the very best of them all! (See page 112)

The Soaring Eagle flew great; HOWEVER, after a few flights the wings snapped and broke when opening. I turned it into a fixed wing glider and piggybacked it on a large rocket.
(See page 107)

Another type of glider is like the Astron Falcon. It goes up like a rocket, with a fixed wing design. Once the engine pops out, the rocket becomes a glider. They can be unstable if everything isn't perfect. The engine is in the top of the rocket. When it discharges and pops out of the rocket, the center of gravity is balanced for it to become a glider.

A rocket glider like the Astro-Blaster is in a different category of rocketry. It goes up like a rocket and then one must glide it back down by remote control. This is not for the beginner.

Gliders are not for the faint of heart.

HELICOPTOR: *Gyroc* takes off like a rocket and once the engine pops out, it becomes a helicopter and rotates safely down to the ground. It works great with small engines; HOWEVER, a C6-3 is like drag racing a Chevy Vega with an oversized engine. It's just a little too much horsepower for a stable flight.

A larger, more dynamic model is the *Helio Copter*. The nose cone is a folded-up helicopter. When it pops off of the main body of the rocket, the rocket comes down with a parachute, while the nose cone becomes a helicopter and rotates down to the ground. They're fun, but we've had rotors break off more than once.

ROCKET COMPANIES: Years ago there was Centuri and a few others, but Estes has always been the frontrunner for great kits and engineering. Quest is a newer company and they have some nice rockets, but Estes has the best name in the business. Throughout the book, most all kits are Estes unless otherwise noted. Any rocket referred to can be investigated by simply searching on the Internet. Many of Estes catalogs can be studied at estesrockets.com. Most of the others have websites also.

This book is not directed toward high-tech advanced rocketry. Using engines exceeding the Estes E class are not covered for the reason that I have no experience with such monstrosities. They are in a league of their own. For me to elaborate on them would require a B.S. degree. (B.S. meaning Bull S#*%.)

"Thou shalt not forget to use thy wadding…or thou will wish thou didist!"

WADDING: The fire resistant wadding sold by Estes is great. A cheap fix, if you've just finished insulating your attic, is to use a small piece of fiberglass insulation; HOWEVER, make sure you collect all of your wadding and especially your little chunks of insulation so as not to litter the environment. The drawback with insulation is that if you rub your eye accidentally after working with it, you'll wish you'd never used it.

I found out the hard way to take a piece of wadding and carefully push it, with the launch rod, into the engine casing area above where the engine goes. It keeps excessive heat from clogging up and collapsing the body tube leading up toward the parachute; HOWEVER, make positive it fits loosely, because it has to blow up through the tube to help release the parachute or streamer. My Saturn five completely closed up and needed to be rebuilt because of the heat generated from those powerful D engines. Had I pushed that piece of wadding directly ahead of the engine it would have absorbed some of the heat and propellant spray.

Stick with the wadding!

If you forget the wadding you'll be reminded in a hurry when seeing your parachute half melted. The Bandit is unique, since it has a muffler system to dissipate the heat and requires no wadding.

INTERNET SEARCHES

If you want to have fun, get on the Internet and do a Google search of most anything you're interested in. Putting in the name of a rocket will usually give a choice of videos to watch. They're fantastic!

Chapter Three
FAVORITE ROCKETS

(This is only a portion of the ones that I've built over the years.)

"Let's light this candle!"
Alan Shepard in *The Right Stuff*

ALPHA 3

This was the first rocket we launched. It's a very nice first rocket, with a plastic fin unit. It never left the launch pad on its third flight. The B4-4 engine blew a hole in the side of the rocket; nevertheless, it was a durable piece of equipment and still flyable. We logged nine launches with "A" and "B" engines before coming to grips with the fact that the time had arrived to move on to a C6-7. I gave it a goodbye kiss, just in case the wind decided not to cooperate. There was no wind at ground level. The rocket took off and went very high. Next we watched it coming back down for a while and then the puff of smoke and an opened chute…and then we watched it drift into the next county. There was a strong wind at 800 feet.

"Thou shalt not use big engines on small rockets until thou are ready to lose them!"

ASTROCAM

What a challenge!

The kit comes in pieces and must be built. The nose cone is a 110 camera. One must be very meticulous when building it; HOWEVER, the finished result is an outstanding camera for taking shots from the air. I launched it with different engines. The B4-4 performed the best. The C6-7 goes very high; HOWEVER, it picks up a lot of speed by the time the parachute opens and that's a recipe for a shredded recovery system. I replaced the 12-inch parachute with an eighteen-inch that I cut a hole in the top of for a faster descent. The 12-inch was shredded from the C6-7. The B4-2 only gives one a picture of the clouds. I shot it off a few times and had the film developed, because I wasn't sure if it worked. The pictures came out fine.

The next time I went out to the field, we used the Altitrak on one of the launches with the C6-7 and it went 280 feet. I was having so much fun that I didn't want to quit launching it and paid dearly for such a dreaded decision. On its seventh launch, once the parachute opened, it drifted into the top of a very high tree. That really hurt; HOWEVER, it was my own fault because it was a windy day.

I couldn't help it. I had to have another! This time I was very careful, launched it a number of times and came up with some great pictures. One secret is to launch it at a little bit of an angle in order to help it flip and also to get a picture of the area you're interested in. If shot straight in the air, there is no telling where it will point once it flips.

After 17 successful flights it was time to set the AstroCam on the shelf. It had done its job.

BANDIT

Bandit's muffler system was ingenious. The inside of the rocket body tube has a number of tubes with holes in them, so by the time the heat given off of the engine reaches the parachute, it's cooled off enough so that the parachute isn't damaged. There was no need for wadding and it was a very reliable and stable rocket. After 22 launches the Bandit was still in good shape.

BIG BERTHA

Hands down, one of the greatest rockets ever built!

It wasn't too small, because it easily used an 18-inch parachute. It wasn't too big for the reason that you could have a successful launch with an "A" engine. If one were to go all the way to a C6-7, there was still a good chance of a fruitful recovery because it never went out of sight and the 18-inch parachute was easy to keep an eye on.

My first Big Bertha flew 25 flights and still had some life left in her. One time I shot it straight up with a B6-6 and the chute opened at 20 feet.

Everyone needs a Big Bertha in the arsenal!

BIG BERTHA

CRUSADER Swing-wing

This is the best rocket/glider Estes ever made. It goes up with plenty of stability and once the wing pops out it flies great. The only weakness of the design is the pod fin. It wants to crack from coming down too fast, so I replaced it with a 12-inch parachute.

The best flights were with the B6-4, for the reason that it has time to stabilize; whereas, the

A8-3 engine gets it up high enough to simply function. On its 9th and final flight a C6-5 was used. It was excellent…and I got the rocket back. It went very high and flew for a long time while the kids were trying to chase it as it went one way and then did a 180-degree turned back in the opposite direction. It flew like that repeatedly and the children kept running back and forth.

DUDE

Who has a coin? I must flip it to decide which is my favorite rocket to launch. Oh…never mind…the Saturn 5 has been permanently retired and the Space Shuttle deserves a rest. Have you ever seen a rocket that was over seven-foot tall leave the launch pad?

The idea was something I never thought about. A Mylar balloon, shaped like a rocket, with a framework for strength. It uses a D12-3 engine and a special launch rod. The air MUST be very calm. If there is any wind at all the rocket will tip over. I had no idea of what we were in for.

UNBELIEVABLE! It went about 300 feet in the air and came down perfectly. We had to do it again. The next launch was as good as the first; HOWEVER, the rocket started loosing air. I'd swear I packed everything the best I could, but there is a lot of heat in the area of the engine and the body of the rocket is simply a Mylar balloon.

I'd already gotten my money's worth, so I wasn't disappointed. A few weeks later we took it out again. I tried to patch the bad spot with the repair kit but it never made a difference, so we took the air compressor tank to the field. After filling it with air, the rocket would stay firm for about fifteen minutes. That's plenty of time to pump it up and get it on the launch pad.

The third launch was perfect.

How often do you get to see a rocket that big take off?

FOUR DUDES

FLYING SAUCER

When's the last time you attended a Roswell Convention? The kit is a lot of fun. It can be shot off from a very small field because it goes straight up and then comes strait down, and is a very durable rocket.

It's a real showstopper!

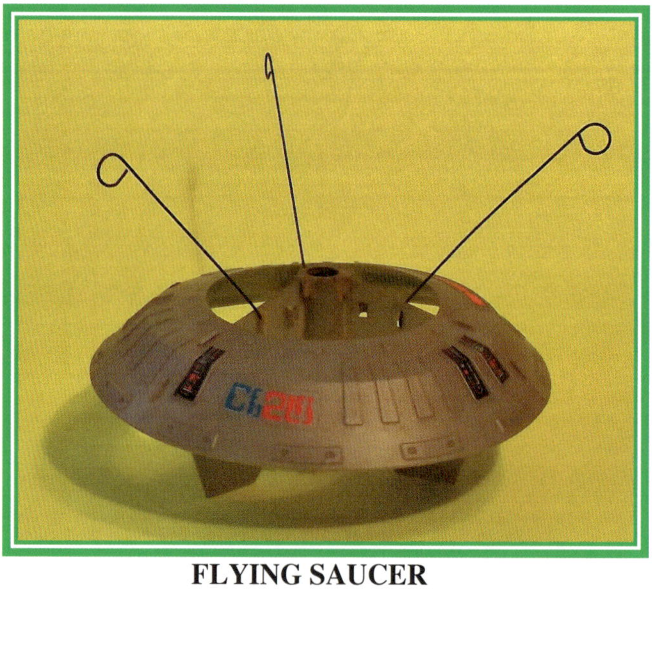

FLYING SAUCER

It goes straight up, flips, and lands like this.

GALACTIC TAXI

The Taxi is one of the prettiest rockets I've ever seen. The problem is that it's heavy and the small body tube can only hold a twelve-inch parachute that fits rather tightly into the rocket. It took a beating on most landings and I liked it so much that I didn't want a busted up memory, so the Galactic Taxi sits on the retirement shelf and is no longer taking passengers.

GALACTIC TAXI

GYROC

Gyroc is a fantastic rocket. I got 19 launches out of mine and that little rocket is still on the shelf. It flew great with most of the engines, but when I shoved a C6-3 in it, the rocket sort of cork screwed into the air. It's very durable and a great concept.

GYROC

JAVALIN

This was our second rocket. It popped apart in the middle and a streamer came out, so one could spot it for recovery. The first launch, with an A3-2T, was great. It went very high. The next launch didn't go quite as well.

The streamer probably fused to the body, because I forgot to use wadding and it didn't came apart. We never saw where the rocket landed because it was getting dark and should have never been shot off, but as with many things in life, I was impatient.

CAPTAINS LOG: Star date 2114.3, "Engine number two isn't working very well. Someone forgot the wadding. Have Scotty see me when he gets off a his smoke break."

LOGIX

Radio Shack had an educational kit of aviation. I built an airplane and there were a number of other things in the box that were interesting. They had one rocket to build that was a very basic one, similar to the Estes Alpha. Using an "A" engine, the rocket went very high and we watched it drift off into the sunset once the parachute opened.

It was a real flash in the pan!

MARS LANDER

Hands down, one of the greatest rockets ever designed, flown, observed, photographed…and one of the hardest to build.

It took the 19th mission for this one to end up on the retirement shelf and it was only because

of extremely flawed experimentation that the Mars Lander had seen its day in the sun.
(See page 111)

I used every recommended engine there was and it flew great with all of them and then I shot it off on a day, devoid of wind, in hopes of a perfect landing. (Perfect referring to it not toppling over when the wind would blow on the parachute once it touched down.) Elation rose throughout the camp when we accomplished that wonderful feat.

MAXI ALPHA 3

The first launch was with a C6-3. Of course it wasn't recommended, but I thought the rocket could handle it. I was wrong. It hit the ground before the parachute could slow the rocket down completely, wrinkling the top of the body tube and breaking a fin. Taping the fin securely to the rocket, with some masking tape, made the Maxi Alpha 3 ready to hit the launch pad again.

Earlier I mentioned that Estes did a fine job recommending engines for rockets. They did not recommend a "C" engine. This was not another one of my "mad scientist" moments. I didn't want to lose the rocket.

The next launch was with a D12-3. It was great and I couldn't believe how high it went. I never cared for the decals on the rocket so I did my own custom decal and paint job. Once I got it back on the workbench, I glued the fin back on with airplane glue and it was as good as new.

The Maxi Alpha 3 is the perfect "big rocket."

MEAN MACHINE

It was six feet long…until on the third launch, when a faulty C6-3 engine only lifted it 50 feet off of the ground. It landed hard and crumbled up very severely and then the parachuted popped out while it was lying on the ground. I had a "D" to "C" engine adaptor. I knew I'd loose it with a "D" engine."

The rocket was rebuilt by cutting out the ruined portion of the body tube and reducing its length to around four feet.

"Dear Lord, please don't let me f#^ up"*
Alan Shepard before taking off in the Mercury Redstone

MERCURY REDSTONE

It went 40 feet in the air with an A8-3, 100 Feet with a B6-4, and probably over 200 feet with a C6-5. It is durable, reliable, and good looking while sitting on a shelf after 18 missions.

There is no end to imagination!

MINI MARS LANDER

That little rascal looks exactly like the Mars Lander, only smaller. The only drawback is that they didn't offer identical looking decals, so it would look like a miniature Mars Lander. Originally it was built with the paint scheme on the picture and then I repainted it and called it "Mini-Me-Mars-Lander."

It flew a number of missions and was a dependable rocket. Every now and then we fire it up again.

MARS LANDER and MINI-ME

MLAS Quest Mars Lander

MLAS is their version of a Mars Lander and it's a very good kit, with a completely different design. After I replaced the shock chord with fifty pound fishing line, it worked great.

On the first launch the lightweight shock chord snapped. The rocket body came down fine because of the parachutes, but the nose cone fell down with a thud. Once I used the fishing line, everything worked perfectly.

50 pound fishing line is also great for hanging up models and rockets.

NINJA

Another nice kit for a small rocket! We had two successful launches and then the launch pad fell over on the third. Rockets don't go very far when they're lying on there side in the grass. One of the drawbacks of the lightweight tripod stands (porta pad) is that they can fall over. That's why I prefer the lantern battery launch pad.

RIGAL 3

The Rigal 3 was a gorgeous rocket and flew well, except when two-staging. This is when I came up with my idea of leaving the fin units behind. It's designed so that there is a gap between the booster engine and the main engine. The booster never fired the main engine, so it bounced off of the ground extremely hard. Not to be redundant…what a pretty rocket!
(See TWO-STAGING page 110)
SAFETY NOTE: Do not leave booster fin units off of short rockets!

SATELLITE KILLER

This is an extremely exciting, good-looking…DANGEROUS rocket.

The Satellite Killer is made by Centuri and is built like a tank. The rocket is very heavy and unstable. On the first launch, with a C6-3, it went about sixty feet high while going 100 feet laterally and nose-diving. There was no damage to the rocket or the spectators.

The next launch was a little better. It landed on the blacktop and still sustained no damage. The third and last launch of its career was scary. It took the launch rod with it while going 40 feet in altitude with an arching trajectory traveling about 40 feet laterally. It nose dived into the ground, with the launch rod still attached.

Someone could have gotten hurt badly on that adventure. It looked like Sylvester Stallone at the end of *Rocky*. I patched it back together, hung it in the garage, and swore to never launch "The Killer" again.

"Thou shalt duct tape, or masking tape
the launch rod to thy
lantern battery launch pad!"
(Sometimes God repeats the laws
in the Old Testament.)

CAPTAINS LOG: Star date 2117.4, "Spock,
I don't think I heard you right. What did you
say happened to the launch rod?"

SATURN FIVE

"This rocket is one small step for man…one giant leap…and a few wrecks for mankind."

Most rocketeers progress from a little Alpha 3, to the Big Bertha, then maybe the V2 or something of the sort; HOWEVER, when this baby sits on the launch pad, it is pure excitement.

On its first launch I used the cluster of 3 "C" engines. I'd had enough of clustering, so after the maiden flight I permanently switched to the singe "D" engine casing. Estes made it so that the rocket could be shot off with either one.

The second launch didn't go so well. Estes wanted to make it scaled looking, so it has fins that are too small for stability in flight. Their solution was clear plastic fins that slipped over top of the rocket fins during a launch. They cocked the rocket without my awareness, so it was stuck on the launch pad.

Remember how we mentioned that the lantern battery launch pad was the best because it is very sturdy and stable? It didn't budge an inch—not even while handling the Saturn Five. I had already replaced the thin blast shield with my own that was bigger and made of 1/8-inch steel.

3,2,1, ignition…have you ever seen the power of a D12-3 when it goes—nowhere? The rocket never left the pad because it was cocked and the engine just kept burning. Once the show was over, not only did it burn a hole through the 1/8 inch steel plate, it kept burning and put a hole into the battery.

I was astonished. The battery wasn't phased!

An executive decision was made; reliability is more important that looks. I glued a set of fins in between the original fins. If I ever build another Saturn Five, I'll make it with larger fins.

After that *hellish* experience the decision was made to *religiously* sand and oil the launch rod before launching rockets, and to set a spacer, or whatever it takes, so that the rocket doesn't cock on the launch pad. (This book is written so that you can learn from my mistakes. I'm not going to make you give me a piggyback ride through the swamp, or handle snakes, but if you plan on facing Darth Vader, or launching rockets off, I'd like to continue your training.)

The next launch went okay except, only one of the 24-inch parachutes opened. The area for the parachutes is very restrictive. The 10-inch parachute on the nose cone gets out of the way without incident, but to squeeze two 24-inch parachutes into the top of the rocket is a lot of material. I made another executive decision to cut one chute off and take my chances with a hard landing. The rocket is built very durable, and with the heavier fins it could sustain a harder landing. Usually a fin would break; nevertheless, it was always easy to repair.

If I ever build another Saturn Five, I'll make it break apart at the main body tube, so that there will be plenty of room for the parachutes.

The next repair was made after a number of launches. The body tube that leads up from the engine was almost completely closed and distorted because of the heat from the "D" engines. I was able to force another tube through it and from then on, I shoved a piece of wadding through the engine area, so that it would absorb the heat and propellant of the engine. The repair was a success. (See page 110 for the two-stage experimentation.)

It had been through many wars and rebuilt over and over. Obi Wan Kenobi said that Vader was more machine than man. My Saturn Five was more hot glue gun and spare parts than the original kit.

Last year I got the itch to fire it one more time. It had been 26 years since that special rocket had sat on the pad. 3,2,1, blastoff. It corkscrewed a little as it climbed about 200 feet into the air. The parachuted deployed, the shock chord broke, and it came down like a brick. Launch number 12 was surely the last. It took forever to get it in good enough shape to put it back on the shelf; specifically for looks and nostalgia. I never considered the fact that the shock chord would be dry rotted.

I love that rocket!

CAPTAINS LOG: Star date 2114.5, "Sulu forgot to replace the shock chord on the shuttle craft. We are taking it out of his paycheck."

SATURN FIVE
Notice the plastic fins.

SCORPION

The Scorpion was a very basic rocket and the workhorse of my multi-staging launches. I bought the starter kit and that's how I came upon the lantern battery launch pad.

Another positive thing about basic, stable rockets is that a person can launch them on a windy day, into the wind, and usually have a successful recovery. I would shoot this one directly into the wind. There was one launch when it went about 500 feet in the air, over a neighborhood, on a 25 degree angle, and returned almost exactly where we were standing.

It went to that place in the sky for lost rockets on its ninth flight with a C6-7 engine.

It sure did fly high!

SCOUT

The scout managed to rack up 21 missions before finding a resting place somewhere in the world that has still not been disclosed to this day. It goes very high with a "C" engine. The Scout logged a number of missions until the day it never returned while using a C6-3.

The rocket is a one of a kind with its tumble recovery. The engine pops down from the engine casing (body tube), but can't eject, because of a hook, so it causes the rocket to tumble, thereby creating an enormous amount of drag. Our first launch ended with a nosedive. The rocket didn't catch on the hook, so I bent it a little and from then on we were in business. Over time I had to reinforce the hook to the body and the biggest secret is to paint it florescent orange in order to have a chance of finding it out in the field or in someone's backyard.

SCRAMBLER

Another fantastic kit! This one was launched five times with "B" and "C" engines and flew great each time. We never broke an egg. I took masking tape and wrapped it around the payload section to insure that it wouldn't come apart. Launching it with a B4-2 engine gave it that realistic liftoff, due to the added weight.

SCISSOR WING TRANSPORT

The Scissor Wing Transport is a rocket glider. I've always loved that kit. Everything must be built perfectly and the elevator needs to be set just right or it can easily end up as "the master *in* a disaster."

I should have never shot the rocket off! It was a very windy day. The B6-2 shot it up in the air and the wing didn't open, so the wind got a hold of it and took it about a hundred yards into a neighborhood and then the wing opened right before it was about to come down. That was enough to make it completely impossible to track because it flew off into a wooded area, never to be seen again. I almost cried.

CAPTAINS LOG: Star date 2114.6, "I asked Scotty if he saw where the glider went. He said…what glider?"

I had to have another!

I made sure everything was perfect…including the weather. With an A8-3 it flew great. I added a clay weight to the tail section so it would glide strait and level. That bird had four perfect launches in a row and then on the fifth one, the B4-2 was faulty and blew the body tube wide open. It never left the pad. I patched it up and set it on the retirement shelf. (See page 133)

SOARING EAGLE

It flew perfect on the first few flights and then every time it was launched, one of the wings would snap. After repairing it repeatedly, once it had reached the ninth flight, I rebuilt it as a fixed-winged aircraft, glued launch lugs on the enormous Old Yeller, 1/8-inch dowel pins on the glider, and piggy backed it for three more launches. It was spectacular! When the parachute opened on the big rocket, the jerking motion gave it enough of a nudge that the glider popped right off and flew down to perfection. (See PIGGYBACKING page 107)

The Soaring Eagle may have been more durable if the wings were made from a stronger wood.

SPACE SHUTTLE

33 launches is a milestone! What a fantastic rocket!

This is one of the best kits Estes ever made. It performs great with the B4-2, B4-4, C6-3, and C6-5 engines. I finally glued the fin units permanently in place to increase the performance and reliability. It's a real workhorse! The glider always flew great and the parachute has plenty of room, so it deployed perfectly each time.

This kit is not for the novice. Plenty of patience and care must be taken with each step. (See Space Shuttle page 112)

SPACE SHUTTLE

Space Shuttle with its special made stand after gluing the fins in place for increased reliablilty.

CAPTAINS LOG: Star date 2114.7,
"Space…the final frontier…"

STAR SHIP ENTERPRISE

"To go where no man…or woman…or child…or dog…has gone before."

I don't believe it's possible to market a more beautiful rocket. Not only is it almost the exact same size as the AMT plastic model, the finished product really does fly.

The design is outstanding, with the long rocket tube to give it stability. We launched it twice with a B6-2, held our breath, watched it fly perfectly, and then carefully caught it on the way down. After two launches my nerves couldn't take any more and I retired it by hanging it from the ceiling by my HO train layout.

It is simply too magnificent to be torn up and we all know, if you launch them enough times they'll eventually get busted up. There is no way the Enterprise could survive a nasty crash. Like the Space Shuttle, working with vacuforms is an adventure. The only thing harder than building things out of vacuforms—is repairing them.

U.S.S. ENTERPRISE

It's hanging from 50 pound fishing line. Notice the rocket tube is painted sky blue to blend in with the wall. Those World War Two airplanes don't have a chance against photon torpedoes.

TORNADO

The tornado is a great little rocket, but it lands very hard. The fin unit and main body break apart and both pieces fall to the ground, with the main rocket-body spinning, so it doesn't land too hard. We had three successful launches and there was at least one broken fin each time.

V-2

Another workhorse of the industry! If you don't have one, it's time to get one. It flies well with anything from a B4-4 to a D12-5.

V-2

WE HAVE LIFTOFF

WIZARD

This was a beautiful rocket, with its decals and purple paint. The streamer was too tight for the body tube and it never came apart. It was lost on its maiden flight, never to be seen again. (It was getting dark.)

Don't be afraid to cut a few inches off of a streamer if it fits too tightly into the body tube!

"Thou shalt not shoot off rockets when it is getting dark!"

Chapter Four
THE EDGE OF THE ENVELOPE
It's All Up In Smoke!

"It is not a simple matter to differentiate unsuccessful from successful experiments. Most work that is finally successful is the result of a series of unsuccessful tests in which difficulties are gradually eliminated."
Dr. Robert H. Goddard

After building over a hundred rockets and more than 800 launches, with many of them being prototypes, it literally is a case of being "All up in smoke!" And worth every penny and hour spent, with what is one of the greatest hobbies in the world.

Quit while you're ahead! That's what I should have done.

With paper, pen, messy handwriting, and incorrect spelling; for the first time in my life, in 1985, I wrote an article. Sending it to *Model Rocket Magazine*, I had hopes of getting it published. Approximately one year later—they published the article. I could honestly say that every article I'd ever written had been published. Furthermore, every article I'd ever submitted in my life had been published. I could have stopped then and considered myself to be a huge success.

The article discussed in detail, dozens of the research and development testing experiments that I'd performed with the model rockets. Model Rocketry is a wonderful hobby. The most exciting thing is the fact that the technology used to build and launch the model rockets, is the same fundamental technology that the space program was built upon. The miniature Space Shuttle was intended to be a single stage rocket. I developed it into a multi-staged vehicle. There were two specific rockets that were about two feet tall when purchased. I turned those two kits into an impressive four-foot rocket. The article documented my work and I was sure they'd appreciate it. I made one enormous oversight. I didn't take time to explain that I was a research development mechanic and did testing on prototypes for a living. Most of my experimental launches were done early in the morning when no one was around. In my own personal way I was respecting the safety code in regards to pre-launch testing.

The president of *Model Rocket Magazine* wrote a reply letter informing me that I had broken six of the "fourteen point safety code" for Model Rocketry. The editor for the magazine also wrote informing me that I should be ashamed of myself for breaking seven of the fourteen points of that same safety code; moreover, I was a menace to the public. At least I received a response; nonetheless, it sure wasn't what I'd expected. (I'm positive that I didn't break rule number eleven on page 92. It refers to climbing telephone poles and retrieving rockets that have their parachutes stuck in high-powered wires.)

My letters of reply to both gentlemen was very apologetic. I informed them that I'd had no intention of embarrassing them, especially of doing anything unsafe. I was a professional research and development mechanic for a manufacturing company and a responsible adult. I used caution and attempted to be as safe as possible when performing experimental launches. The letter was finished with, "I'm sorry, please forgive me, and thank you for your time.

To my complete surprise, months later I received a letter thanking me for my outstanding article. Not only that, but they requested that I write a follow-up article on my experimentation of reducing drag on rockets in relation to the different finishes. Also enclosed were five copies of the magazine with my article, and a gift certificate for Estes rocket supplies so I could continue my research projects.

I was elated at the situation; even so, I couldn't stop laughing at the state of affairs. The editor must have worked overtime editing my article so that it didn't come across as being irresponsible. And I appreciated the fact that never once did he say anything derogatory such as "David J. Petry is a mad scientist that should be banned to Australia and not permitted to snorkel at the Great Barrier Reef."

Here is the article as it appeared in Model Rocket Magazine. It is well written but somewhat different than the original submission.

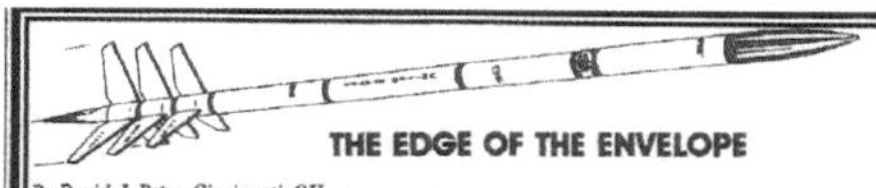

THE EDGE OF THE ENVELOPE

By David J. Petry, Cincinnati, OH

Have you ever launched a rocket in a field that was too small or three-staged a single-stage rocket? I am thirty years old, and I have been doing model rocketry for four years. In junior high school some of my friends did model rocketry. I always kept up with the space program, but for some reason the small rockets did not catch my interest.

Four years ago, while Christmas shopping for our two boys, I saw the model rockets and bought a starter kit knowing absolutely nothing about the hobby. Since then I have built sixty rockets, half of them scratch-built prototypes, and logged almost four hundred flights.

There was a movie released a few years ago called "The Right Stuff". It told the story of a few men who had what it takes to become an astronaut. The few men who had "the right stuff" were military test pilots. These men flew their aircraft and took them to "the edge of the envelope" to see the maximum capability of the aircraft. There was at that time, and still is today, one place above all others where men with "the right stuff" take their aircraft to "the edge of the envelope" and sometimes outside the edge and sometimes right into the ground. This place is Edwards Air Force Base.

To me the most enjoyable part of model rockets is taking my rockets to "the edge of the envelope", and, when I am tired of that, I take them "outside the edge". Some of your readers are probably the type who value their rockets to the point that they will not risk losing them. Let's face it, with the cost of a rocket, not to mention hours of time making it look good and fly well, most people play it safe and never try a risky launch.

Well, if you are this type, just sit back, relax, and have a good laugh at the writer of this article, who eventually just has to take that rocket over the edge. Do not misunderstand me. I always follow the Safety Code, but I still love to experiment.

I built the Scout. This is a small, tumble recovery rocket. I had launched it a few times with 1/2A and A engines. Nothing risky. If you have this rocket, you know how high it will go. I live in Cincinnati, OH, and we do not have many good launch fields. If you are lucky, you have a whole field to yourself without soccer and baseball games, and then you may still have trouble getting rockets back. I took the Scout, painted it fluorescent orange. Back to the field we went. A8-3; no problem. B6-4; we saw the rocket the entire flight. Should we try the C6-5? Go for it! We never saw the rocket after the tracking smoke. I thought for sure we had lost the rocket, but we finally found it 12" outside the woods.

My favorite rocket of all is the Estes Space Shuttle. This is not only a good looking model, but it works perfectly. I really took my time with this rocket because I knew it had to be built just right to work right. Estes recommends a C5-3 or C6-3 engine. Both of these engines worked beautifully. Estes says the model looks like the real thing, and I can say after twenty-two flights with mine, I still agree with their statement. What about a C6-5 engine? (Editor--At this point he is considering breaking rule 2 of the Model Rocketry Safety Code. His further activities come under rule 12 of the Code. Rule 12 deals with research activities and requires that all launches of unproven designs or methods be conducted in complete isolation from persons not participating in the actual launching.)

I made sure everything was perfect and that the launch rod was straight up and down because with a five-second delay, I knew there was no room for error. Off it went with a C6-5 and then the moment of truth. At about seventy feet above ground, the parachute opened on the rocket. The orbiter took off and glided down for another perfect launching. "Roger, Houston. We have a touchdown."

Let's not stop there. What about B6-2? What about B4-2? Both engines worked perfectly. On to bigger and better things. Let's try to two-stage our Space Shuttle for more altitude. Don't think I enjoy losing rockets or watching them go into the ground. I almost cried when I lost my first AstroCam rocket. I got over being anxious one day and launched it with a C6-5 engine at a launch site that was too small. Counting rocket, camera, and film, I was out almost thirty dollars and that does not include the hours of time spent building the camera. But where would we be if Chuck Yeager had looked at the X-1 rocket plane and said "I'm not getting in that flying bomb."?

Back to the two-stage shuttle launch. The big day is here, and we are ready with a C6-0 booster engine and a 1/2A-4 engine for the second stage. Talk about a spectacular flight. Words cannot describe it. We had taken a rocket made for a C5-3 or a C6-3 engine and tested it successfully with other engines and successfully two-staged it. (Editor--Remember that the writer is an adult with four years of model rocketry experience. He always follows the Safety Code in his research activities.)

Moving on to even bigger and better things, I scratch-built a beautiful D-Powered rocket. It was four inches in diameter and three feet tall. I spent hours on this rocket. To begin with, I wanted to do an air drag test. I left the balsa nose cone and fins unfinished and painted the rocket with flat paint. Just think about the drag of a homemade balsa nose cone four inches in diameter! The rocket was launched with a D12-3 and reached an altitude of one hundred feet. It was really neat to see this big rocket slowly lift-off and watch the D engine pouring out smoke. For our next test we needed to verify our altitude, so we launched the rocket two more times. Both times it reached an altitude of about one hundred feet.

I took the rocket and sanded it and used five coats of balsa sealer on the nose cone and fins. Then I painted the rocket with high gloss paint. I took Pledge and waxed the rocket before launching it. Off to the launch site I went. I sanded the launch rod and rubbed a small amount of light oil on it. The big rocket was launched, and I could not believe my eyes when we tracked it at 235 feet. More than twice as high as before! We launched it again to verify our results, and it went over two hundred feet again.

The question to be asked is not "Do I have the Right Stuff?". Many people, I am sure, think I am crazy. The question is, "Does a specific rocket and a specific flight have the Right Stuff to be a success or to bring the fun and satisfaction to a person that a hobby is supposed to give?". I get a special feeling inside every time I see a real rocket take off, and model rocketry is the closest thing I know of to bring me that same feeling. Maybe one day I will be less adventurous, but for now, I wonder if I could turn my Estes Saturn Five into a rocket glider?

Perfect launch photo of Marc Tawey's (Westport, CT) Honest John.

6 MRN MAGAZINE SUMMER '87

This is the original article as it appeared in Model Rocket Magazine.

Unless you're a rabbit, the print may be too small to read, since it's been shrunk down to fit in a six-by-nine paperback. Here is a re-typed copy of the article for your reading pleasure.

THE EDGE OF THE ENVELOPE
By David J. Petry, Cincinnati, Ohio
1987

Have you ever launched a rocket in a field that was too small, or three-staged a single-stage rocket? I'm thirty years old, and been doing model rocketry for four years. In junior high school some of my friends were into that hobby. I always kept up with the space program, but for some reason the small rockets didn't catch my interest.

Four years ago, while Christmas shopping for my two boys, I saw the model rockets and bought a starter kit knowing absolutely nothing about the hobby. Since then I've built sixty rockets, half of them scratch-built prototypes, and logged almost four hundred flights.

There was a movie released a few years ago called *The Right Stuff*. It told the story of a few men who had what it takes to become an astronaut. The few men who had "the right stuff" were military test pilots. These men flew and took their aircrafts to "the edge of the envelope" to see the maximum capability of the aircraft. There was at that time, and still is today, one place above all others where men with "the right stuff" take their aircraft to "the edge of the envelope"—sometimes outside the edge, and other times right into the ground. That place is Edwards Air Force Base in California.

To me the most enjoyable part of model rockets is taking them to “the edge of the envelope” and when I’m tired of that, I take them “outside” the edge of the envelope. Some of the readers are probably the type who value their rockets to the point that they will not risk losing them. Let’s face it, with the cost of a rocket, not to mention hours of time making it look good and fly well, most people play it safe and never try a risky launch.

Well, if you are that type, just sit back, relax, and have a good laugh at the writer of this article, who eventually just has to take that rocket over the edge. Don’t misunderstand me. I always follow the Safety Code, but still love to experiment.

I built the Scout. This is a small, tumble recovery rocket. I had launched it a few times with 1/2A and A engines. Nothing risky. If you have this rocket, you know how high it will go. I live in Cincinnati, Ohio, and we don’t have many good launching fields. If you’re lucky, you’ll have the whole field to yourself without a soccer or baseball game, but then you may still have trouble getting your rockets back.

I took the scout and painted it fluorescent orange. Back to the field we went. A8-3; no problem. B6-4; we saw the rocket the entire flight. Should we try the C6-5? Go for it! We never saw the rocket after the tracking smoke. I thought for sure we had lost it, but we finally found it 12 inches outside of the wooded area.

My favorite rocket of all is the Estes Space Shuttle. This is not only a good-looking model, but it works perfectly. I really took my time with this rocket, because I knew it had to be built just right to work. Estes recommends a C5-3 or C6-3 engine. Both of these engines worked beautifully. Estes says that the model looks like the real thing, and I can say after twenty-two flights with mine, I still agree with their statement. What about a C6-5 engine? (Editor – At this point he is considering braking rule 2 of the Model Rocketry Safety Code. His further activities come under rule 12 of the code. Rule 12 deals with research activities and requires that all launches of unproven designs or methods be conducted in complete isolation from persons not participating in the actual launching.)

I made sure everything was perfect and that the launch rod was straight up and down because with a five-second delay, I knew there was no room for error. Off it went with a C6-5 and then the moment of truth. At about seventy feet above the ground, the parachute opened on the rocket. The orbiter took off and glided down for another perfect launch. "Roger Houston. We have touchdown."

Let's not stop there. What about a B6-2? What about a B4-2? Both engines worked perfectly. On to bigger and better things! Let's try to two-stage our Space Shuttle for more altitude. Don't think I enjoy losing rockets or watching them go into the ground. I almost cried when losing my first AstroCam rocket. I got over anxious one day and launched it with a C6-5 engine at a launch site that was too small. Counting rocket, camera, and film, I was out almost thirty dollars and that doesn't include the hours of time-spent building the camera. But where would we be if Chuck Yeager had looked at the X-1 rocket plane and said, "I'm not getting in that flying bomb?"

Back to the two-stage shuttle launch. The big day is here, and we are ready with a C6-0 booster engine and a 1/2A-4 engine for the second stage. Talk about a spectacular flight. Words cannot describe it. We had taken a rocket made for a C5-3 or a C6-3 engine and tested it successfully with other engines and successfully two-staged it. (Editor – remember that the writer is an adult with four years of model rocketry experience. He always follows the Safety Code in his research activities.)

Moving on to bigger and better things. I scratch built a beautiful D-powered rocket. It was four inches in diameter and three feet tall. I spent hours on this rocket. To begin with, I wanted to do an air drag test. I left the balsa nose cone and fins unfinished and painted the rocket with flat paint. Just think about the drag of a homemade balsa nose cone four inches in diameter! The rocket was launched with a D12-3 and reached an altitude of one hundred feet. It was really neat to see that big rocket slowly lift-off and watch the D engine pouring out smoke. For our next test we needed to verify our altitude, so we launched the rocket two more times. Both times it reached an altitude of one hundred feet.

I took the rocket and sanded it and used five coats of balsa sealer on the nose cone and fins.

Then I painted the rocket with high gloss paint. I took Pledge and waxed the rocket before launching it. Off to the launch site I went and sanded the launch rod before rubbing a small amount of light oil on it. The big rocket was launched, and I couldn't believe eyes when we tracked it at 235 feet; more than twice as high as before! We launched it again to verify our results, and it went over two hundred feet again.

The question to be asked is not "Do I have the Right Stuff?" Many people, I'm sure are thinking that I'm crazy. The question is, "Does a specific rocket and a specific flight have the Right Stuff to be a success or to bring the fun and satisfaction to a person that a hobby is supposed to give?" I get a special feeling inside every time I see a rocket take off, and model rocketry is the closest thing I know of to bring me that same feeling. Maybe one day I will be less adventurous, but for now, I wonder if I could turn my Estes Saturn Five into a rocket glider?

Chapter Five
EXPERIMENTATION

"Research is what I'm doing
when I don't know what I'm doing."
Wernher von Braun

"Thou shalt pay attention to thy safety code
and if doing experimentation,
thou shalt be very careful!"

NAR MODEL ROCKET SAFETY CODE

1. **Materials.** I will use only lightweight, non-metal parts for the nose, body, and fins of my rocket.
2. **Motors.** I will use only certified, commercially made model rocket motors, and will not tamper with these motors or use them for any purposes except those recommended by the manufacturer.
3. **Ignition System.** I will launch my rockets with an electrical launch system and electrical motor igniters. My launch system will have a safety interlock in series with the launch switch, and will use a launch switch that returns to the "off" position when released.
4. **Misfires.** If my rocket does not launch when I press the button of my electrical launch system, I will remove the launcher's safety interlock or disconnect its battery, and will wait 60 seconds after the last launch attempt before allowing anyone to approach the rocket.

5. **Launch Safety.** I will use a countdown before launch, and will ensure that everyone is paying attention and is a safe distance of at least 15 feet away when I launch rockets with D motors or smaller, and 30 feet when I launch larger rockets. If I am uncertain about the safety or stability of an untested rocket, I will check the stability before flight and will fly it only after warning spectators and clearing them away to a safe distance. When conducting a simultaneous launch of more than ten rockets I will observe a safe distance of 1.5 times the maximum expected altitude of any launched rocket.
6. **Launcher.** I will launch my rocket from a launch rod, tower, or rail that is pointed to within 30 degrees of the vertical to ensure that the rocket flies nearly straight up, and I will use a blast deflector to prevent the motor's exhaust from hitting the ground. To prevent accidental eye injury, I will place launchers so that the end of the launch rod is above eye level or will cap the end of the rod when it is not in use.
7. **Size.** My model rocket will not weigh more than 16 ounces at liftoff and will not contain more than 125 grams (4.4 ounces) of propellant or 320 N-sec (71.9 pound-seconds) of total impulse.

8. **Flight Safety.** I will not launch my rocket at targets, into clouds, or near airplanes, and will not put any flammable or explosive payload in my rocket.
9. **Launch Site.** I will launch my rocket outdoors, in an open area at least as large as shown in the accompanying table, and in safe weather conditions with wind speeds no greater than 20 miles per hour. I will ensure that there is no dry grass close to the launch pad, and that the launch site does not present risk of grass fires.
10. **Recovery System.** I will use a recovery system such as a streamer or parachute in my rocket so that it returns safely and undamaged and can be flown again, and I will use only flame-resistant or fireproof recovery system wadding in my rocket.
11. **Recovery Safety.** I will not attempt to recover my rocket from power lines, tall trees, or other dangerous places.

The modern code doesn't list it; HOWEVER, when I did my testing they had fourteen rules. Listed as number 12 and sometimes as number 14 was: Pre-Launch Test – When conducting research activities with unproven designs or methods I will, when possible, determine their reliability through pre-launch tests. I will conduct launchings of the unproven designs in complete isolation from persons not participating in the actual launching.

"If mankind feared trying new things, we wouldn't have ice cream or airplanes."
David J. Petry

DESIGN OF THE MONTH CONTEST WINNER

HARRIER JET ROCKET

Estes Design of the Month winner

Making something take off like a rocket, but come down horizontally and land like a Harrier fighter jet was a monumental task—but it worked!

Using the Estes "Futuristic Parts Assortment" designer's kit, I built what is actually a basic rocket; HOWEVER, the nose cone of the main body is glued to the body tube and the fins of the rocket, on touchdown, become horizontal landing gear. The hard part was plugging up the body tube of the rocket at just the right spot and then having a slit in the body of the rocket that lined up with the piggyback body tube that carried the parachute. When the burst of air from the engine pops the nose cone off, it's the nose cone attached to the piggyback tube that deploys the parachute and brings the Harrier down vertically.

It performed perfectly during its three flights. Two with "B" engines and one with a C6-5; HOWEVER, the landing gear broke a little on each flight.

The solution is to build it with a larger diameter, piggyback body tube, so a bigger parachute can be used.

I built a second generation Harrier Jet Rocket that was larger and it flew great, right up until an engine caught the rocket on fire. It resulted in some fantastic photographs.

Model rocketry is exciting!

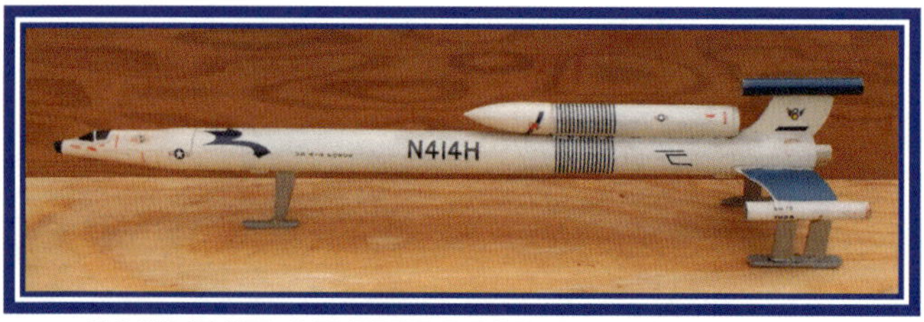

CONTEST OF THE MONTH HARRIER

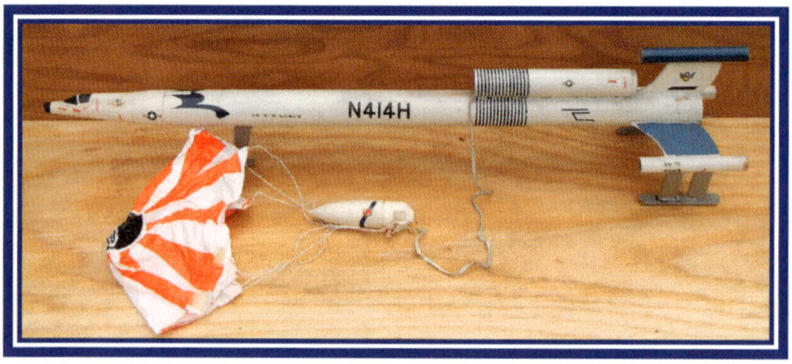

The parachute pops out of the piggyback body tube. It goes up like a rocket and comes down vertically.

E2 HARRIER

This was the second generation that took off like a rocket and came down like a harrier jet. The E2 was bigger and had a number of successful launches until the one that became a great photo-op. It looks like a scene out of *The Right Stuff.*

I had a C6-0 booster engine and a C6-5 main engine. The rocket shot up like "a bat out of hell," but instead of the main engine firing, there was a delay. The rocket was now positioned horizontally and then the booster engine exploded, caught the back of the rocket on fire and the main rocket ignited.

I'm not really sure of what happened, so I'll let the pictures do the talking and you can figure it out for yourself. It was worth it to get the photos. Fighter pilots have mishaps all the time.

E2 HARRIER

The rocket caught fire from the booster engine and was traveling vertically when the main engine fired. It was exciting! And great for a photo shot.

This was a different day when everything went the way it was supposed to. Rockets perform better when there aren't engine malfunctions.

DESIGN OF THE MONTH
Honorable Mention

TWIN SUPER FLEE

Two body tubes glued together and two engines firing! It received an honorable mention from Estes design of the month contest. The rocket used a featherweight-streamer recovery system with the body tubes breaking apart half way up and each one had its own streamer. It was a cluster launch of two 1/2A-2T engines. Both propelled it up and then both popped open the body tubes. It performed three perfect launches in a row.

Far left is the Twin Blaster. It was clustered with an engine in each side and didn't work very well.

The tall, skinny one is the U.S.S. Super Flea. It was three staged and flew up, then across the field and finally straight into the ground.

On the right is the Honorable Mention Twin Super Flea. It performed very well on every launch.

MOON LANDER

WARNING: Children, don't try this at home…or anywhere else!

"Thou shalt not launch rockets without a launch lug…EVER!"

"These are the voyages of the…"

I had to try it and was very careful, making sure that no one was around, but at the same time was ready to do a little Bruce Lee defense move if it came at me.

The rocket was a prototype that resembled the Mars Lander. It took a while to make the nose cone because of its 3 ½ inch diameter. The base was very secure so that it would sit flat on the ground. 3,2,1, blastoff—and it did a Rainbow-arch maneuver, with a maximum altitude of about 30 feet and hitting the ground hard with a nose dive. One fin was broken and the parachute was melted.

Rockets need launch lugs!

CAPTAINS LOG: Star date 2114.8, "One of those guys wearing a red shirt asked if they could launch a rocket without a launch lug. I tried to be patient when I asked him, "Are you out of you Vulcan mind?"

CENTER OF GRAVITY CENTER OF PRESSURE

MIGHTY BEN "D"

Estes recommends that a person should tie a string around the rocket and spin it in a circle to see how stable it is. Had I done that to this prototype, it would have been a disaster. The rocket was very unstable because I didn't add a heavy nose weight to the nose cone. Unlike the Mosquito, this one was longer and had a parachute.

Always make sure that the center of gravity and center of pressure are at a good relationship to each other, and always do the lasso test of spinning the rocket around in a circle before the maiden flight of a scratch built rocket.

"Thou shalt not cluster a rocket with the engines far apart!"

TWIN BLASTER

A catastrophe waiting to happen!

The twin blaster was a two-engine cluster rocket, with one engine in each side. It took off, but was very unstable. The rocket had a wide, flat surface and was heavy, so it didn't fly without incident. The thrust must be in the middle of the rocket to insure a stable flight.

It was rebuilt with one engine in the middle. I got a batch of bad engines and it had a few nosedives because the engines never released the burst to pop open the nose cone. The rocket was durable and survived seven launches with 1/2A-2T and A10-3T engines. Number eight was from our back yard. It was caught in a tree and impossible to recover.

The rocket was beautiful and flew very high; nevertheless, it was so bottom heavy that it didn't want to flip over during a launch and the streamers didn't create enough drag to insure a soft landing. The body tubes were so tiny I couldn't use a parachute.

DRAG

RECORD ALTITUDE ROCKET

How much difference does a good finish make in regards to altitude? This rocket was built for that very purpose. True science must include controlled experiments. A few flights with a rough, un-sanded finish gave an average altitude of 205 feet. Once sanded and having the added weight of a number of coats of primer, paint and high gloss paint, while being sanded between coats...well, it was slicker than a baby's bottom with baby oil rubbed on it.

It went 255 feet.

BIG DADDY

Big Daddy flew great with a D12-3. I shot it off with a C6-3 and it opened just in time to keep from being damaged. With the D12-3 it flew three or four times higher than with the C6-3. Rockets of the same weight with smaller diameters fly much higher. That reveals how larger diameter surfaces cause much higher friction in the air than smaller sized body tubes.

BIG DADDY

M.A.C.

The rocket was big and heavy, with a 4 inch diameter body tube and nose cone. I made it from a mailing tube and turned the balsa nosecone on my homemade lathe. Originally built with a dull finish, I recorded launches using D12-3 engines and consistently recorded an altitude of 100 feet. After sanding and refinishing the rocket with primer and high gloss paint it flew to an altitude of over 200 feet.

That's INCREDIBLE!

Model Rocket Magazine wanted me to do an article on drag performance, but I was too busy at the time to send one in. Maybe some day I'll do precise analyses of drag and finishes and submit a detailed article.

GLIDERS

SOARING EAGLE became a fixed winged aircraft after a number of mishaps with the wings snapping. Since it naturally had a nice dihedral of the wings, because it was light and the wings flexed upward, it flew for a long time. I wondered if I could piggyback it on a large rocket and still get some flights out of it. The "Old Yeller" was a real heavyweight and, by leaps and bounds, the best candidate for such an election. It worked great and so did the glider. I was surprised at how perfectly stable the launches were, in spite of the entire wing surface being exposed during the thrusting stage of the launches. (see page 107)

SOARING EAGLE

The Soaring Eagle flew perfectly unless a wing snapped.

ASTRON FALCON IMITATION was scratch built from a picture in an old Estes catalog.

I tried to duplicate the Estes Astron Falcon. It launched okay, but did a nosedive and went on the disabled list after one inning…or was it one launch? Apparently I didn't figure it out completely.

I consoled myself while reflecting on Thomas Edison and his failures with the light bulb.

On the far left is the Mercury Redstone, with the custom made payload section, ready to take a number of astronauts into outer space. (One of them is Big Bird.) On the right is my attempt at making the Astron Falcon from a picture in the catalog. It was "Span in the can."

PIGGYBACK TRANSPORT

OLD YELLER

Estes quit making the Colossus, so I had to build my own by combining the V2 kit with the Phoenix missile. It resulted in a very durable, highly reliable finished product.

Old Yeller was launched 12 successful times in a row. On a calm day it would actually go up 60 feet with a C6-3 and there was just enough time for the chute to open. It was like watching the soldiers come out of the back of the C-130 Hercules when their parachutes open with just enough time to soften the landing. It was great for launching at a small field, since it was big; HOWEVER, when using a D12-3 it went 400 feet.

I started using a D12-5 when I turned it into the Old Yeller Space Shuttle, since it piggybacked the Soaring Eagle glider for one great flight after another. The jarring of the parachute opening up was enough to cause it to release the glider.

SCISSOR WING TRANSPORT
OLD YELLER
CRUSADER
All ready to launch!

On the far left and right are the Scissor Wing Transport and the Crusader, ready to glide across the sky.
In the middle is Old Yeller chomping at the bit to take Soaring Eagle for a ride.

"A-okay full go."
Alan Shepard

MULTI-STAGING

SCORPION

This is an Estes kit; however, it's listed under "Prototypes" because of the three-stage experimentation. When a rocket is long and stable, like the scorpion, one need not use fin units for the booster rockets. All that is required is to tape the booster engines to the main engines with a thin layer of tape and then make sure that the main engine snaps into place with the engine hook by breaking through the tape.

The day I used two "A" boosters with a 1/2A was very interesting. It was a hot, sticky, July afternoon. There was no wind at ground level. I shot it strait up. It went extremely high as all three engines fired successfully…the chute opened…and it took forever for it to land…three feet in front of me.

It went to that place in the sky for lost rockets on its ninth flight, with a C6-7 engine. Wow! It sure did fly high!

RIGAL 3

It flew well with a B4-4 and was an eye-catching rocket; HOWEVER, when moving on to a two-stage launch using the booster stage fin unit, it was designed with a gap between the booster engine and the main engine. The result was a crash, since the main engine never fired, causing the rocket to fall from the sky and get busted up a little.

That mishap gave me the idea of multi-staging rockets without booster fins. It is only successful if the rocket has enough length so that the center of pressure and center of gravity are in the correct relationship.

I was ready to take a chance of losing it with a three stage launch using a "C" booster for the first stage, an "A" booster for the second stage and a B6-6 for the main engine. The flight was great and I was shocked when we recovered it. Two of the kids ran for a long distance to find it. If we hadn't launched it 20 degrees into the wind we would have never seen it again.

MARS LANDER

It took the 19th mission for this one to end up on the retirement shelf and it was only because of extremely flawed experimentation that the Mars Lander had seen its day in the sun.

There were two questions to be asked: "What is the dark matter in the universe" and "Is it possible to two stage the Mars Lander?"

The big day had arrived. (I knew I'd need to do a "Lone Ranger" launch to be safe, so I was by myself.) The booster rocket was a C6-0 and the main engine a B4-2. The weather was calm. 5,4,3,2,1, blastoff!

It went 30 feet in the air and started doing cartwheels without ever leaving a two-foot radius. When all of the engines had fired and burnt out, it fell to the ground, was smoldering and then the parachute popped out.

After many hours of repair, it looked good enough to put on the retirement shelf.

CAPTAINS LOG: Star date 2114.9 "The Mars Lander cannot be successfully two staged. If I catch Lieutenant Ohura doing that again there'll be hell to pay."

SPACE SHUTTLE

All one needs to do is tape the booster engine to the regular engine. I used a C6-0 booster and a 1/2 A-3 and another time it was launched with a B6 booster and a C6-3. It went very high. I always got it back because the orbiter would fly in a circling pattern, so it didn't drift off.

The rocket flew very stable on each flight. The secret is to make sure the fin units are in the correct position. I insured it by gluing them in place and making a stand for the shuttle to sit on.

U.S.A. SUPER FLEA

Built similar to a Super Flea, this rocket was much longer with a break apart, feather weight recovery because it was intended to be a three stage rocket and I wanted to get it back.

The first two—two-stage launches were fine, so it was time to for an official three stage adventure. More bad engines! The A10 booster engines delayed igniting the second and third stages. It made for an interesting flight. The rocket reached an altitude of about 150 feet, leaned at a ninety degree angle, the second engine fired and it thrusted sideways for about 100 feet. After all of the fuel was discharged it pointed nose first at the ground and then the main engine fired and it powered four inches into the ground…and then when the parachute was supposed to deploy, the charge blew the engine out of the rocket about 50 feet into the air.

M.A.C.

Another rocket built from mailing tubes!

I turned the huge nosecone with my homemade lathe fixture and glued some heavy-duty fins on it. The rocket was very dependable and durable, because the body tubes were extremely thick.

I don't think Estes stole my idea on purpose, because they had given me an honorable mention award and a contest of the month award; HOWEVER, a year after I submitted this rocket to Estes for the design of the month, they never acknowledged it, but released it as "Bailout." (They used a much smaller rocket, but the idea of having action figures parachute out of the rocket was submitted by me.)

I would take G.I. Joe figures, mount 12-inch parachutes to them, wrap them in a few sheets of toilet paper so they didn't get tangled, and launch them into the air. It was spectacular seeing the huge rocket, with a 30-inch chute and 2 or 3 paratroopers wearing 12-inch chutes, descending toward the earth.

Eventually I did a number of two-stage launches with a D-12 booster and a D12-3 for the main engine. The rocket performed great with just a singe "D" engine.

Launch number 9 was interesting. I wanted to recover it and the field (as always) wasn't as large as I would have preferred, so I played it safe and used a D-12 booster with a D11-9 engine. The flight was stupendous until the descending phase of the mission as it raced downward, toward a wooded area. Nine seconds is a long delay and a heavy rocket can pick up an enormous amount of speed with each passing second. The nose cone never had a chance of popping open. You could hear branches breaking when it slammed through the trees. It was a tank with fins.

There were some kids watching the launches and they scurried into the woods and recovered it. I took the pieces home and patched the poor thing up. It didn't sustain much more damage than a few broken fins and a big gouge in the nose cone.

The next launch was to be one of the biggest ever. The Cincinnati area is not overly friendly to the hobby of model rocketry. There are trees and power lines everywhere. The rocket was completely rebuilt, refinished and sitting on the launch pad with two "D" boosters and a D11-9 inside the rocket. This was my first "D" powered, three-stage launch and I already accepted the fact that I may never see the M.A.C. again.

3,2,1, liftoff! It grunted a little and reached an altitude of about eighty feet and then the second booster kicked in. It shot up at least another 200 feet and then the third one fired and it was nearly out of sight. The sound was incredible…and then it started coming down…and kept coming. The rocket was going so fast that the discharge couldn't blast the nose cone off. It was screaming by the time it slammed into the ground.

At least we got it back.

There was a considerable amount of damage; nevertheless, as we said before, it was a flying tank and worth every busted piece to experience one of my favorite launches ever.

There was more life left in the old boy and it made it to launch number 16 before a tree grabbed a hold of it and wouldn't let go.

M.A.C. lifting off with three "D" engines. The ignition system was the car battery. It was a perfectly stable flight.

M.A.C. ready to go with 3 "D" engines and needing no fin units.

SATURN FIVE

It was time to two-stage the Saturn Five. All systems were go. The booster was taped to the main engine using my simple two-stage technique without fins, and it was all I could do to contain the excitement.

3,2,1, blastoff…or not? The booster blew up, lifted the rocket three inches off of the launch pad, and ignited the main engine. It shot up and flew well; nevertheless, the parachutes wouldn't deploy properly and it nose-dived. We almost ordered a hearse, but I was not going to put the Saturn Five out to pasture without giving her a chance to avoid the glue factory. I had a gut feeling she had another race left in her.

Just like in the movie *Son of Frankenstein*, I had to bring that creature back to life again…and did!

Hoping it was just a fluke, the next flight was almost identical…and so were the repairs. Figuring the whole batch of booster engines were bad, I put the last one in a vise on the workbench, wired it up with an igniter and hit the switch. It blew up like the others.

The rocket had now been rebuilt a number of times and each rebuild was more of a challenge. The hot glue gun was working overtime. The next flight went fine except it cork screwed a little. The Saturn Five had a lot of miles on it.

NONSTANDARD PARTS

MOSQUITO D

For years I worked around all types of machinery. We would use a multitude of tooling. The end mills came in cardboard tubes. They were very heavy-duty. I made a number of rockets out of them over the years. The Mosquito D was a large version of the little Mosquito rocket, with a D12-7 engine and featherweight recovery. It went very high and was never recovered. That's the problem when there is no streamer or parachute.

The combination of end mill tubes, mailing tubes, and the Estes designer's kits, I was able to make many prototypes.

I had made a fixture that would hold a bulk chunk of balsa wood. I then held it in the drill press, and the combination of files and different grits of sandpaper, I was able to make my own nose cones and adapter pieces. (See page 125)

MOSQUITO C

The mosquito C was the same as the Mosquito D, but had a smaller diameter. It was powered by a C6-7 engine and also had a featherweight recovery system. The rocket went very high and it's a good thing I didn't spend too much time on the finish because that flight went literally out of sight…forever.

MOSQUITO D2

Have you ever watched the footage of the first Redstone and Atlas rockets when the United States first entered the space race? One after another they either fizzled out, blew up on the pad, or exploded shortly after takeoff. And so did the Mosquito D2. It was basically the same as the first generation. The first launch had a faulty engine. The rocket only went 100 feet in the air, ran out of gas, flipped and went into a nosedive. Before hitting the grassy field, the discharge shot it six inches into a muddy spot in the ground.

It didn't seem to have sustained any damage, so we launched it again. Unbeknown to us, the engine block ring to keep the engine from going up into the body had become detached. The engine took Mosquito D2 very high and went up inside of the rocket tube. When it came back to earth the body tube was burnt up, with the rocket completely destroyed.

U.S.S PETRY

Height 8 feet, 42-inch parachute recovery

The U.S.S. Petry was a beast. The eight-footer was made from mailing tubes and was very heavy. They are very thick. It demanded a cluster of three D12-3s and a 42-inch parachute made from heavy plastic. The launch was spectacular! How often do you see and hear three "D" engines firing at the same time? It reached an altitude of 150 feet and was so heavy that it started to come down fins first. The parachute popped out and U.S.S. Petry landed safely with only two broken fins.

Six months later was its second and final voyage. The launch was another success; HOWEVER, the parachute wouldn't open and it hit the ground very hard. We sent it to a resting place of hanging on the wall of the garage. Where else does one store an 8-foot rocket?

DAVID J. PETRY with the U.S.S. PETRY
I almost didn't recognize him without the gray, thinning hair.
Notice the fin taped to the body tube.

ONE WAY MISSIONS

Shooting rockets off from the backyard is a recipe for never getting them back. I had three mini engines and really felt a need to shoot off a few rockets. It was a dreary, misty, windy day.

I went out to the workbench and made some fins, sawed off the end of a few balsa nose cones, grabbed a few launch lugs from out of a designer kit and glued all of the pieces to the engines with a heavy dab from the hot glue gun. They had now become official Mosquito rockets without a body tube.

Those little rascals were fired off into the sky and flew perfectly. Just as I pick up used bottle rockets in my back yard on the fifth of July, I imagine somebody found these in their back yard. It had rained all morning, so there was no chance of a fire hazard.

PAYLOAD SECTIONS

X-RAY

If you're going to collect rockets you must have a model of the X-RAY in your arsenal; even if you never shoot a grasshopper off into space.

Enough said!

MURCURY REDSTONE

We put a 10-inch parachute on an army man, wrapped toilet paper around him, and loaded him in the body tube. It looked spectacular seeing the main chute for the rocket body, the parachute for the capsule, and then the army man floating down.

Eventually, I tied the capsule to the body tube shock chord and used an 18-inch parachute like a regular rocket. The capsule is very realistic and I got tired of repairing the rocket gantry.

I made a huge payload section that fit the body tube of the Redstone rocket. It was interchangeable with the mercury capsule and accomplished by using a fishing lure quick-change clip. The nose cone and body tube adapter were turned on my homemade lathe, and the clear section was an end mill holder from the shop. The kids loved it because I'd load up their Fisher Price plug people and shoot them off into space. The extra weight gave us a realistic liftoff with a "C" engine.

REDSTONE ROCKET WITH PAYLAOD

These are different tools that I made to tighten onto a chunk of balsa wood, to be put into a drill press and very carefully turned into nose cones and adapters.

If you attempt such a venture, make sure to wear a dust mask, safety glasses and be very careful not to push too hard, because the balsa chunk can fly out of the fixture. It seemed that overall; extra-course sandpaper removed it very well.

Cut as much stock off of the chunk as you can ahead of time.

This is not for the novice. I did special machine shop techniques for thirty-two years.

MERCURY REDSTONE
With the Lantern Battery Launch Pad

RECOVERY SYSTEMS

COBRA

The Cobra was a very reliable rocket and had a few accidents. It was a shorter version of the Mean Machine and a little less than five-feet long. Eventually I rebuilt it with a mid body break-apart recovery and a smaller parachute, so it was easier to get back. Break-apart recovery lessens the chance of broken fins and crinkled bodies.

We flew it eleven times and then I was ready to say goodbye to it, if that was what fate had in store for us. Using my technique of a booster engine, without a fin unit, I taped a C6-0 booster to a C6-7 and we were ready to put it out of sight.

It flew very high, and the only reason we recovered it was because of the new, break apart recovery with a smaller parachute.

U.S.S. PETRY 2

Missing my eight-foot U.S.S. Petry, I built a ½ scale model that was four-foot long. Since it was so tall and of such a basic design, after 12 launches with all different engines, the U.S.S Petry 2 was still flyable. The last flight was a huge success. It went completely out of sight with a B6 booster and a C6-5 main engine. I still can't believe it was recovered! Its salvation was the mid-section break-apart recovery.

SPIN FIN ROCKETS

Estes makes a standard "Spin Fin" and it works great. Over the years I decided to make bigger ones. Build the kit the standard way, but when it comes to the fins, make them smaller and glue them on at a slight angle like the "spin fin" rockets.

Quest makes a Big Betty and it works well as a spin fin. Their rockets are good, less expensive and have a few different engineering designs than Estes; HOWEVER, they aren't quite as heavy duty, but well worth buying.

The interesting thing about a spin fin is that on a windy day, the spin gives it stability and endurance against the wind. The drawback manifests itself once the parachute opens. The rocket spins and the shock chords of the parachute get very twisted. The reason the spin gives it more stability is for the same reason that rifling gives a bullet a higher level of accuracy.

It's worth painting the rocket with alternating colors because it enhances the spinning as it lifts off into the sky. Once you build a bigger spin fin, the little one may feel left out while it sits on the shelf, for the reason that you'll never want to fly it again.

SPIN FIN MADE FROM BIG BETTY

Notice the angle of the fins.

"There was a demon that lived in the air. They said whoever challenged him would die. Their controls would freeze up, their planes would buffet wildly, and they would disintegrate. The demon lived at Mach 1 on the meter, seven hundred and fifty miles an hour, where the air could no longer move out of the way. He lived behind a barrier through which they said no man could ever pass. They called it the sound barrier."
Narrator at the beginning of *The Right Stuff.*

X-1 ROCKET

Chuck Yeager: *"Hey Ridley, make another note here, would ya? Must be something wrong with this ol' Mach meter. Jumped plumb off the scale. Gone kinda screwy on me."*
Jack Ridley: *"You go ahead and bust it, we'll fix it. Personally, I think you're seein' things."*
Chuck Yeager: *"Yeah, could be. But I'm still goin' upstairs like a bat outta hell."*

Dialogue from *The Right Stuff*

This was built to look like the X-1 aircraft that Chuck Yeager flew when he broke the sound barrier. I was happy with the final look but in retrospect it should have been built to fly on top of a good sized rocket like the X-20 Dyno-Soar project. It fluttered a lot and was unstable. It managed to survive four flights with low powered engines and now sits on the retired wing of the shelf.

X-1 SOUND BARRIER ROCKET

Chapter Six
THE DEAD SEA SCROLLS OF ROCKETS
Where Rockets Retire

Years ago, Diane and I took a trip to the Holy Land. Driving down to the Dead Sea, we saw the caves where a shepherd boy, one day by accident, found the Dead Sea Scrolls.

Nothing lives in the Dead Sea. The salt content is so concentrated that a person can't sink regardless of how hard they try, and nothing worth talking about lives there.

This literary work has been titled *Bible of Model Rocketry*. It's a guide and hopefully your journey has helped you find some truths in regards the hobby of model rockets. It's only appropriate that we call the graveyard, or resting place of one's model rockets, The Dead Sea Scrolls of Rockets.

Enjoy the photographs!

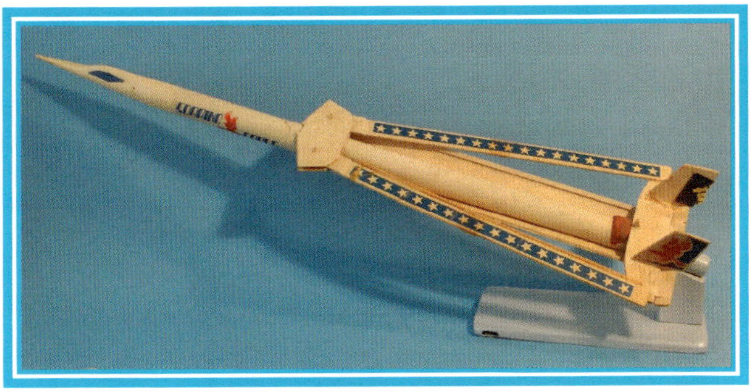

SOARING EAGLE

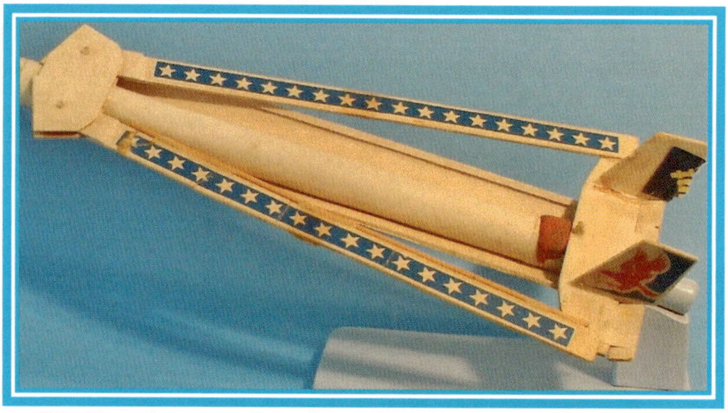

Notice the wooden dowel and glue at the top of the wing. Also take note of the red, clay weight by the tail section.

SCISSOR WING TRANSPORT

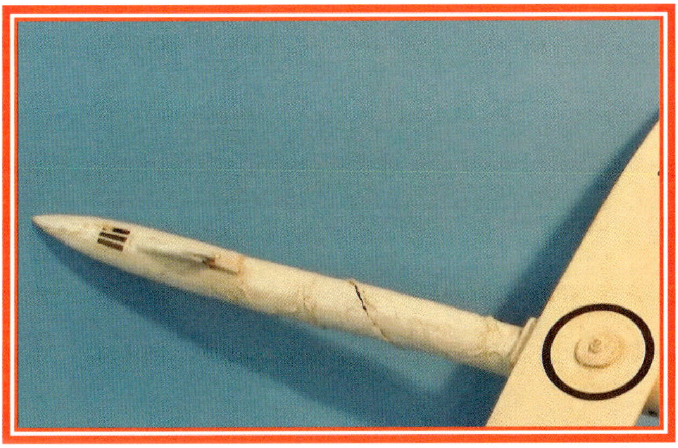

I almost cried. The engine blew up and completely ripped the body tube apart on the launch pad.

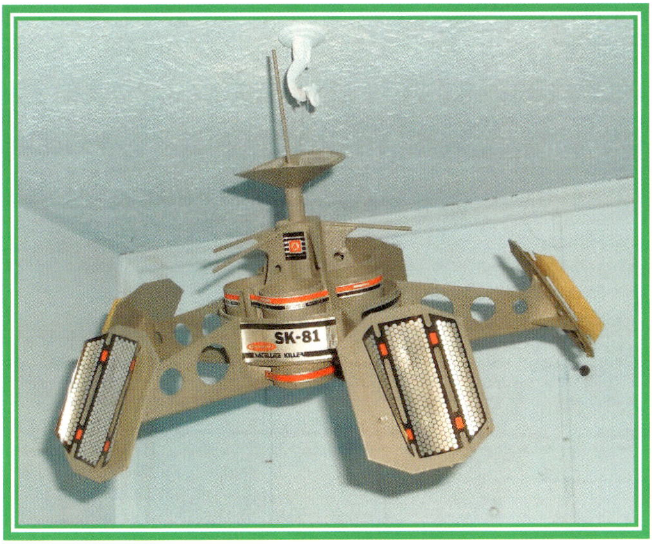

SATELLITE KILLER
It was appropriately named!

SATURN FIVE
After surgery

This reminds me of the Starship Enterprise when it was dry docked after the battle in *Wrath of Khan*.

Those fins may not be pretty but they're very dependable and practical.

A FEW ROCKETS

MARS LANDER

"Houston…we have a problem."

EPILOGUE

Watching Alan Shepherd being launched into space, and the Gemini capsule, with astronauts doing the space walk, followed by Neil Armstrong walking on the moon saying, "That's one small step for man, one giant leap for mankind," gave me a special feeling down deep in my loins that has never left. Every time I launch one of those rockets I get that same feeling I had as a youngster those many years ago.

We can't help but grow older physically; HOWEVER, becoming a grouchy, old, narrow-minded complainer is a choice made by many—but not by me. We can become better or bitter as we grow old. Some folk make a conscious decision that they're right and everyone else is wrong. Those folks have limited their happiness by not being willing to let loose and enjoy life.

I have chosen to be better, enjoy life, and to make the most of each day. Building and flying model rockets is an enjoyable thing to do. If people think it's childish, let them think that. I find the opposite to be true. Men and women will say, "You do that? Let me know the next time you shoot them off. I'd love to see it."

In reality, building and launching rockets is rather sophisticated and it's truly for the thinkers of the world…nevertheless, we won't let those outsiders know that. Don't worry about what other people think. If playing golf, or going to the casino (with limited amounts of money), or sitting in five-degree weather watching football makes you happy, then do it! Life is short and we only get to go around the "block of life" one time, so make the most of it.

John Glen, in *The Right Stuff* looked out the window of the Friendship 7 capsule and said something that sums up my outlook on having the hobby of model rocketry. "The view is tremendous."

"Mystery creates wonder and wonder is the basis of man's desire to understand."
Neil Armstrong

A FEW MORE ROCKETS

20673094R00078

Made in the USA
Charleston, SC
19 July 2013